The Essence of Spinoza's
Ethics

The Essence of Spinoza's *Ethics*

Edited with an Introduction by
Hunter Lewis

Revised and updated version of an
original translation from the Latin by
R. H. M. Elwes

AXIOS

The Essence of... series of books are edited versions of great works of moral philosophy, distilled to reveal the essence of their authors' thought and argument. To read the complete, unedited version of this work, and see the excised passages, please visit our website at www.AxiosInstitute.org.

Axios Press
P.O. Box 118
Mount Jackson, VA 22842
888.542.9467   info@axiosinstitute.org

For a complete list of all of Spinoza's Propositions, Notes, Corollaries, Definitions, Axioms, and Postulates referenced but not included in this book, please see our website: http://www.AxiosInstitute.org/bookstore/ The Essence of Spinoza's Ethics/Uncut Text.

Library of Congress Cataloging-in-Publication Data

Spinoza, Benedictus de, 1632-1677.
[Ethica. English]
The essence of Spinoza's Ethics / edited with an introduction by Hunter Lewis; revised and updated version of an original translation from the Latin by R.H.M Elwes.
p. cm.
Some passages have been excised.
Includes index.
ISBN 978-1-60419-056-4 (pbk.)
1. Ethics. I. Lewis, Hunter. II. Elwes, R. H. M. (Robert Harvey Monro), b. 1853. III. Title.

B3973.E5E4 2012

170--dc23

2012023265

Contents

Introduction

Baruch de Spinoza
(1632–1677)*

S PINOZA'S LIFE, AS well as his doctrines, reflects the possibilities of a pure "religion" of deductive logic, where "religion" is defined as a set of personal evaluations and beliefs and actions inspired by those evaluations and beliefs, not just a socially organized religion like Judaism or Christianity. A solitary bachelor, Spinoza moved from town to town to escape the time-consuming attentions of his devoted friends; an imperturbable boarder, he sometimes remained in his room for three months at a time, to

---

* This introduction is adapted from material first printed in Hunter Lewis, *A Question of Values: Six Ways We Make the Personal Choices that Shape Our Lives* (San Francisco: Harper Collins, 1990), 47-50.

the fond amazement of whatever family he was staying with; an expert lens grinder, he always paid his own way and gently declined the financial patronage of princes. As Spinoza explained the motive behind this unconventional existence, which some of his contemporaries viewed as a kind of extreme secular monasticism:

> After experience had taught me that all the usual surroundings of social life are vain and futile, and seeing that none of the objects of my fears contained in themselves anything either good or bad, except insofar as the mind is affected by them, I finally resolved to inquire whether there might be some real good having power to communicate itself, which would affect the mind singly, to the exclusion of all else—whether, in fact, there might be anything of which the discovery and attainment would enable me to enjoy continuous, supreme, and unending happiness.

> I say "I *finally* resolved," for at first sight it seemed unwise willingly to lose hold on what was sure for the sake of something then uncertain. I could see the benefits which are acquired through fame and riches, and that I should be obliged to abandon the quest of such objects, if I seriously devoted myself to

the search for something different and new. I perceived that if true happiness chanced to be placed in the former I should necessarily miss it; while if, on the other hand, it were not so placed, and I gave them my whole attention, I should equally fail.

I therefore debated whether it would not be possible to arrive at the new principle or at any rate at a certainty concerning its existence, without changing the conduct and usual plan of my life. With this end in view I made many efforts, but in vain. . . .

For the ordinary surroundings of life which are esteemed by men (as their actions testify) to be the highest good may be classed under the three heads—Riches, Fame, and the Pleasures of Sense: with these three the mind is so absorbed that it has little power to reflect on any different good. By sensual pleasure the mind is enthralled . . . so that it is quite incapable of thinking of any other object; when such pleasure has been gratified it is followed by extreme melancholy. The pursuit of honors and riches is likewise very absorbing, especially if such objects be sought simply for their own sake. . . . In the case of fame the mind is still more absorbed, for fame is conceived as always good for its own sake, and as the ultimate end to which all actions are directed. Further the attainment of riches and fame is not followed as in the case of sensual pleasure by repentance, but, the more we acquire, the greater is our delight, and consequently, the more we are incited to increase both the one and the other; on the other hand, if our hopes happen to be frustrated, we are plunged into the deepest sadness. Fame has the further drawback that it compels its votaries to order their lives according to the opinions of their fellow men, shunning what they usually shun, and seeking what they usually seek.

When I saw that all these ordinary objects of desire would be obstacles in the way of a search for something different and new—no, that they were so opposed thereto that either they or it would have to be abandoned, I was forced to inquire which would prove the most useful to me. But further reflection convinced me that . . . evils arise from the love of what is perishable, such as the objects already mentioned [while] love toward a thing eternal and infinite feeds the mind wholly with joy, and is itself unmingled with any sadness, wherefore it is greatly to be desired and sought for with all our strength.

[Even then] I could not forthwith lay aside all
love of riches, sensual enjoyment, and fame.
[But] while my mind was employed with [de-
ductive logic], it turned away from its former
objects of desire.... Although these intervals
were at first rare, and of very short duration,
yet afterwards,... they became more frequent
and more lasting.*

After persevering in this highly disciplined existence for many years, Spinoza concluded that the all-
important initial premise, the logical key that would
unlock a complete system of values, could be found
in the concept of perfection. For perfection to be
truly perfect it must be absolute; and to be absolute,
it must exist. From this *a priori* argument (*a priori*
because it is thought to be self-evidently true), one
may infer that God (another name for perfection)
must exist, and one may then proceed, step by step,
through definitions, axioms, and propositions laid
out like Euclid's geometry, to a complete cosmological and ethical system....

Like Spinoza's modest life of humility and retire-
ment, the Spinozan philosophical system might seem
superficially compatible with traditional Jewish or
Christian belief: It places God at the beginning of
the reasoning chain. But unlike systems based on the

---

* *On the Improvement of the Understanding.*

cosmological argument for the existence of God (the observable phenomenon of cause and effect in the universe implies God as a First Cause) or the teleological argument (the organization of the universe implies God as an initial Organizer), Spinoza's ontological argument (to be perfect, God must be) does not necessarily assume a God like that of Judaism or Christianity. Indeed, Spinoza concluded that God was more likely to be the universe (pantheism) than the creator of the universe (theism), and this position led to excommunication from his synagogue, near assassination, and dismissal by a Christian acquaintance as a "wretched little man, [a] vile worm of the earth."

Eventually Spinoza's ontological argument, together with its cosmological and teleological counterparts, was refuted by other philosophers, notably David Hume and Immanuel Kant in the eighteenth century. Thereafter, these logical set pieces lived a kind of half-life, appearing and reappearing, revived, re-refuted, revived again. Even in the 1980s, some contemporary American scientists speculated about an "anthropic principle" that bears a close resemblance to the cosmological and teleological arguments, and toward the end of his life Einstein insisted, "I believe in Spinoza's God." Meanwhile Spinoza's attitude, as opposed to his precise logical technique, has never lost its power to move. As Goethe wrote:

After I had looked around the whole world in vain for a means of developing my strange nature, I finally hit upon the *Ethics* of this man.... Here I found the serenity to calm my passions; a wide and free view over the material and moral world seemed to open before me. Above all, I was fascinated by the boundless disinterestedness that emanated from him. That wonderful sentence "He who truly loves God must not desire God to love him in return" with all the propositions on which it rests, with all the consequences that spring from it, filled my whole subsequent thought.

—HUNTER LEWIS

Book One

On the Improvement of the Understanding

AFTER EXPERIENCE HAD taught me that all the usual surroundings of social life are vain and futile, and seeing that none of the objects of my fears contained in themselves anything either good or bad, except insofar as the mind is affected by them, I finally resolved to inquire whether there might be some real good having power to communicate itself, which would affect the mind singly, to the exclusion of all else—whether, in fact, there might be anything of which the discovery and attainment would enable me to enjoy continuous, supreme, and unending happiness.

I say "I *finally* resolved," for at first sight it seemed unwise willingly to lose hold on what was sure for the sake of something then uncertain. I could see the benefits which are acquired through fame and riches, and that I should be obliged to abandon the quest of such objects, if I seriously devoted myself to the search for something different and new. I perceived that if true happiness chanced to be placed in the former I should necessarily miss it; while if, on the other hand, it were not so placed, and I gave them my whole attention, I should equally fail.

I therefore debated whether it would not be possible to arrive at the new principle or at any rate at a certainty concerning its existence, without changing the conduct and usual plan of my life. With this end in view I made many efforts, but in vain. For the ordinary surroundings of life which are esteemed by men (as their actions testify) to be the highest good, may be classed under the three heads—Riches, Fame, and the Pleasures of Sense: with these three the mind is so absorbed that it has little power to reflect on any different good. By sensual pleasure the mind is enthralled to the extent of quiescence, as if the supreme good were actually attained, so that it is quite incapable of thinking of any other object; when such pleasure has been gratified it is followed by extreme melancholy, whereby the mind, though not enthralled, is disturbed and dulled.

The pursuit of honors and riches is likewise very absorbing, especially if such objects be sought simply for their own sake,* inasmuch as they are then supposed to constitute the highest good. In the case of fame the mind is still more absorbed, for fame is conceived as always good for its own sake, and as the ultimate end to which all actions are directed. The attainment of riches and fame is not followed as in the case

---

* This might be explained more clearly: I mean, by distinguishing riches according as they are pursued for their own sake, or in furtherance of fame, or sensual pleasure, or the advancement of science and art.

of sensual pleasures by repentance, but, the more we acquire, the greater is our delight, and, consequently, the more are we incited to increase both the one and the other, unless our hopes happen to be frustrated, in which case we are plunged into the deepest sadness. Fame has the further drawback that it compels its votaries to order their lives according to the opinions of their fellowmen, shunning what they usually shun, and seeking what they usually seek.

When I saw that all these ordinary objects of desire would be obstacles in the way of a search for something different and new—nay, that they were so opposed thereto, that either they or it would have to be abandoned, I was forced to inquire which would prove the most useful to me. For, as I say, I seemed to be willingly losing hold on a sure good for the sake of something uncertain. However, after I had reflected on the matter, I came in the first place to the conclusion that by abandoning the ordinary objects of pursuit, and betaking myself to a new quest, I should be leaving a good, uncertain by reason of its own nature, as may be gathered from what has been said, for the sake of a good not uncertain in its nature, but only in the possibility of its attainment.

Further reflection convinced me that if I could really get to the root of the matter I should be leaving certain evils for a certain good. I thus perceived that I was in a state of great peril, and I compelled myself to seek with all my strength for a remedy, however uncertain it might be, as a sick man struggling with a deadly disease, when he sees that death will surely be upon him unless a remedy be found, is compelled to seek such a remedy with all his strength, inasmuch as his whole hope lies therein. All the objects pursued by the multitude not only bring no remedy that tends to preserve our being, but even act as hindrances, causing the death not seldom of those who possess them, and always of those who are possessed by them.

There are many examples of men who have suffered persecution even to death for the sake of their riches, and of men who in pursuit of wealth have exposed themselves to so many dangers, that they have paid away their life as a penalty for their folly. Examples are no less numerous of men who have endured the utmost wretchedness for the sake of gaining or preserving their reputation. Lastly, there are innumerable cases of men who have hastened their death through overindulgence in sensual pleasure. All these evils seem to have arisen from the fact that happiness or unhappiness is made wholly to depend on the quality of the object which we love. When a thing is not loved, no quarrels will arise concerning it—no sadness will be felt if it perishes—no envy if it is possessed by another—no fear, no hatred, in short no disturbances of the mind. All these arise from the love of what is perishable, such as the objects already mentioned.

But love towards a thing eternal and infinite feeds the mind wholly with joy, and is itself unmingled with any sadness, wherefore it is greatly to be desired and sought for with all our strength.

It was not at random that I used the words, "If I could go to the root of the matter," for, though what I have urged was perfectly clear to my mind, I could not forthwith lay aside all love of riches, sensual enjoyment, and fame. One thing was evident, namely, that while my mind was employed with these thoughts it turned away from its former objects of desire, and seriously considered the search for a new principle; this state of things was a great comfort to me, for I perceived that the evils were not such as to resist all remedies. Although these intervals were at first rare, and of very short duration, yet afterwards, as the true good became more and more discernible to me, they became more frequent and more lasting, especially after I had recognized that the acquisition of wealth, sensual pleasure, or fame, is only a hindrance, so long as they are sought as ends not as means. If they are sought as means, they will be under restraint, and, far from being hindrances, will further not a little the end for which they are sought, as I will show in due time.

I will here only briefly state what I mean by true good, and also what is the nature of the highest good. In order that this may be rightly understood, we must bear in mind that the terms good and evil are only applied relatively, so that the same thing may be called both good and bad, according to the relations in view, in the same way as it may be called perfect or imperfect. Nothing regarded in its own nature may be called perfect or imperfect, especially when we are aware that all things come to pass according to the eternal order and fixed laws of nature. Human weakness holds us back from attaining to this order in our own thoughts, but meanwhile man conceives a state of mind much more stable than his own, and sees that there is no reason why he should not himself acquire such a state of mind. Thus he is led to seek for means which will bring him to this pitch of perfection, and calls everything which will serve as such means a true good. The chief good then is that he should arrive, together with other individuals if possible, at the possession of the aforesaid state of mind. What that state of mind is we shall show in due time, namely, that it is the knowledge of the union existing between the mind and the whole of nature.

This, then, is the end for which I strive, to attain to such a state of mind myself, and to endeavor that many should attain to it with me. In other words, it is part of my happiness to lend a helping hand that many others may understand even as I do, so that their understanding and desire may entirely agree with my own. In order to bring this about, it is necessary to understand as much of nature as will enable us to attain to the aforesaid goal and also to form a social order such as is most conducive to the attainment of this goal by the greatest number with the least difficulty and danger. We must seek the assistance of Moral Philosophy and the Theory of Education. In addition, as health is no insignificant means for attaining our end, we must also include the whole science of Medicine, and, as many difficult things are by contrivance rendered easy, and we can in this way gain much time and convenience, the science of Mechanics must in no way be despised. But, before all things, a means must be devised for improving the understanding and purifying it, as far as may be at the outset, so that it may apprehend things without error, and in the best possible way.

Thus it should be apparent to everyone that I wish to direct all sciences to one end and aim, so that we may attain to the supreme human perfection which we have named. Whatever in the sciences does not serve to promote our object will have to be rejected as useless. To sum up the matter in a word, all our actions and thoughts must be directed to one end. Yet, as it is necessary that while we are endeavoring to attain our purpose, and bring the understanding into the right path, we should carry on our life, we are compelled first of all to lay down certain rules of life as provisionally good, to wit the following:

1. To speak in a manner intelligible to the multitude, and to comply with every general custom that does not hinder the attainment of

our purpose. For we can gain from the multitude no small advantages, provided that we strive to accommodate ourselves to its understanding as far as possible: moreover, we shall in this way gain a friendly audience for the reception of the truth.

2. To indulge ourselves with pleasures only insofar as they are necessary for preserving health.

3. To endeavor to obtain only sufficient money or other commodities to enable us to preserve our life and health, and in general to follow such general customs as are consistent with our purpose.

Having laid down these preliminary rules, I will proceed to the first and most important task, namely, the amendment of the understanding.

In order to bring this about, the natural order demands that I should here recapitulate all the modes of perception, which I have hitherto employed for affirming or denying anything with certainty, so that I may choose the best, and at the same time begin to know my own powers and the nature which I wish to perfect.

Reflection shows that all modes of perception or knowledge may be reduced to four:

1. Perception arising from hearsay or from some sign which everyone may name as he pleases.

2. Perception arising from mere experience—that is, from experience not yet classified by

the intellect, and only so called because the given event has happened to take place, and we have no contradictory fact to set against it, so that it therefore remains unassailed in our mind.

3. Perception arising when the essence of one thing is inferred from another thing, but not adequately; this comes when from some effect we gather its cause, but without much understanding.

4. Lastly, there is the perception arising when a thing is perceived solely through its essence, or through the knowledge of its proximate cause.

All these kinds of perception I will illustrate by examples. By hearsay I know the day of my birth, my parentage, and other matters about which I have never felt any doubt. But knowledge of this kind can be false. By mere experience I know that I shall die, for this I can affirm from having seen that others like myself have died, though all did not live for the same period, or die by the same disease. I know by mere experience that oil has the property of feeding fire, and water of extinguishing it. In the same way I know that a dog is a barking animal, man a rational animal, and in fact nearly all the practical knowledge of life.

We deduce one thing from another as follows: after I have become acquainted with the nature of vision, and know that it has the property of making one and the same thing appear smaller when far off than when near, I can infer that the sun is larger than it appears, and can draw other conclusions of the same kind.

Lastly, a thing may be perceived solely through its essence; when, for example we know that two and three make five, or that two lines each parallel to a third, are parallel to one another. The things which I have been able to know by this kind of knowledge are as yet very few.

Nevertheless, the fourth mode alone apprehends the adequate essence of a thing without danger of error. This mode, therefore, must be the one which we chiefly employ. . . .

Book Two

The Ethics

Part A
God

I N WHAT FOLLOWS I shall attempt to explain the nature and properties of God. I shall show that he necessarily exists, that he is one: that he is, and acts solely by the necessity of his own nature; that he is the free cause of all things, and how he is so; that all things are in God, and so depend on him, that without him they could neither exist nor be conceived; lastly, that all things are predetermined by God, not through his free will or absolute fiat, but from the very nature of God or infinite power. I have further, where occasion offered, taken care to remove the prejudices, which might impede the comprehension of my demonstrations. Yet there still remain misconceptions not a few, which might and may prove very grave hindrances to the understanding of the concatenation of things, as I have explained it above.

I have therefore thought it worthwhile to bring these misconceptions before the bar of reason.

All such opinions spring from the notion commonly entertained, that all things in nature act as men themselves act, namely, with an end in view. It is accepted as certain that God himself directs all things to a definite goal (for it is said that God made all things for man, and man that he might worship him). I will, therefore, consider this opinion, asking first, why it obtains general credence, and why all men are naturally so prone to adopt it. Secondly, I will point out its falsity; and, lastly, I will show how it has given rise to prejudices about good and bad, right and wrong, praise and blame, order and confusion, beauty and ugliness, and the like.

This is not the place to deduce these misconceptions from the nature of the human mind: it will be sufficient here, if I assume as a starting point, what ought to be universally admitted, namely, that all men are born ignorant of the causes of things, that all have the desire to seek for what is useful to them, and that they are conscious of such desire. Here from it follows, first, that men think themselves free inasmuch as they are conscious of their volitions and desires, and never even dream, in their ignorance, of the causes which have disposed them so to wish and desire. Secondly, that men do all things for an end, namely, for that which is useful to them, and which they seek. Thus it comes to pass that they only look for a knowledge of the final causes of events, and when these are learned, they are content, as having no cause for further doubt. If they cannot learn such causes from external sources, they are compelled to turn to considering themselves, and reflecting what end would have induced them personally to bring about the given event, and thus they necessarily judge other natures by their own. Further, as they find in themselves and outside themselves many means which assist them not a little in their search for what is useful, for instance, eyes for seeing, teeth for chewing, herbs and animals for yielding food, the sun for giving light, the sea for breeding fish, etc., they come to look on the whole of nature as a means for obtaining such conveniences.

As they are aware that they found these conveniences and did not make them, they think they have cause for believing, that some other being has made them for their use. As they look upon things as means, they cannot believe them to be self-created; but, judging from the means which they are accustomed to prepare for themselves, they are bound to believe in some ruler or rulers of the universe endowed with human freedom, who have arranged and adapted everything for human use. They are bound to estimate the nature of such rulers (having no information on the subject) in accordance with their own nature, and therefore they assert that the gods ordained everything for the use of man, in order to bind man to themselves and obtain from him the highest honor. Hence also it follows, that everyone thought out for himself, according to his abilities, a different way of worshipping God, so that God might love him more than his fellows, and direct the whole course of nature for the satisfaction of his blind cupidity and insatiable avarice. Thus the prejudice developed into superstition, and took deep root in the human mind; and for this reason everyone strove most zealously to understand and explain the final causes of things.

But in their endeavor to show that nature does nothing in vain, i.e., nothing which is useless to man, they only seem to have demonstrated that nature, the gods, and men are all mad together. Consider, I pray you, the result: among the many helps of nature they were bound to find some hindrances, such as storms, earthquakes, diseases, etc.; so they declared that such things happen, because the gods are angry at some wrong done them by men, or at some fault committed in their worship. Experience day by day protested and showed by infinite examples, that good and evil fortunes fall to the lot of pious and impious alike; still they would not abandon their inveterate prejudice, for it was easier for them to class such contradictions among other unknown things of whose use they were ignorant, and thus to retain their actual and innate condition of ignorance, than to destroy the whole fabric of their reasoning and start afresh.

They therefore laid down as an axiom, that God's judgments far transcend human understanding. Such a doctrine might well have sufficed to conceal the truth from the human race for all eternity, if mathematics had not furnished another standard of verity in considering solely the essence and properties of figures without regard to their final causes. There are other reasons (which I need not mention here) besides mathematics, which might have caused men's minds to be directed to these general prejudices, and have led them to the knowledge of the truth.

I have now sufficiently explained my first point. There is no need to show at length, that nature has no particular goal in view, and that final causes are mere human figments. This, I think, is already evident enough, both from the causes and foundations on which I have shown such prejudice to be based, and also from Part I, Proposition 16, and Proposition 32, Corollary,* and, in fact, all those propositions in which I have shown, that everything in nature proceeds from

---

* Ed. note: Spinoza breaks the book into Parts, which are indicated by Roman numerals. Within those Parts are various other elements: propositions (indicated by standalone Arabic numerals), notes (indicated by an *n* if there is only one note, or *n1*, *n2*, *n3* and so forth, if there is more than one note), corollaries (indicated by a *c*, followed by a numeral if there is more than one corollary), definitions (*def*), axioms (*ax*), postulates (*post*), and, in one section, specific definitions of emotions (*emot*). So the shorthand reference for "Part I, Prop. 16, and Prop. 32, Corollary" would be "*I: 16, 32 c*," whereas a reference to "*V: 31; I: ax3*" would mean "Part V, Proposition 31, and Part I, Axiom 3."

a sort of necessity, and with the utmost perfection. However, I will add a few remarks, in order to overthrow this doctrine of a final cause utterly. That which is really a cause it considers as an effect, and *vice versa*: it makes that which is by nature first to be last, and that which is highest and most perfect to be most imperfect. Passing over the questions of cause and priority as self-evident, it is plain from I: 21, 22, 23, that that effect is most perfect which is produced immediately by God; the effect which requires for its production several intermediate causes is, in that respect, more imperfect. But if those things which were made immediately by God were made to enable him to attain his end, then the things which come after, for the sake of which the first were made, are necessarily the most excellent of all.

Further, this doctrine does away with the perfection of God: for, if God acts for an object, he necessarily desires something which he lacks. Certainly, theologians and metaphysicians draw a distinction between the object of want and the object of assimilation; still they confess that God made all things for the sake of himself, not for the sake of creation. They are unable to point to anything prior to creation, except God himself, as an object for which God should act, and are therefore driven to admit (as they clearly must), that God lacked those things for whose attainment he created means, and further that he desired them. . . .

Many argue in this way. If all things follow from a necessity of the absolutely perfect nature of God, why are there so many imperfections in nature? Such, for instance, as things corrupt to the point of putridity, loathsome deformity, confusion, evil, sin, etc. But these reasoners are, as I have said, easily confuted, for the perfection of things is to be reckoned only from their own nature and power; things are not more or less perfect, according as they delight or offend human senses, or according as they are serviceable or repugnant to mankind. To those who ask why God did not so create all men, that they should be governed only by reason, I give no answer but this: because matter was not lacking to him for the creation of every degree of perfection from highest to lowest; or, more strictly, because the laws of his nature are so vast, as to suffice for the production of everything conceivable by an infinite intelligence, as I have shown in I: 16.

Such are the misconceptions I have undertaken to note; if there are any more of the same sort, everyone may easily dissipate them for himself with the aid of a little reflection.

· · · · ·

[*The reasoning behind these conclusions is contained in Appendix A. This Appendix begins with Spinoza's famous ontological proof of God's existence.*]

Part B

Mind and Emotion

1.

ALL OUR ENDEAVORS or desires so follow from the necessity of our nature, that they can be understood either through it alone, as their proximate cause, or by virtue of our being a part of nature. . . .

2.

Desires, which follow from our nature in such a manner that they can be understood through it alone, are those of the mind, insofar as the latter is conceived to consist of adequate ideas. The remaining desires are only of the mind, insofar as it conceives things inadequately, and their force and increase are generally defined not by the power of man, but by the power of things external to us. The former desires are rightly associated with actions, the latter passions, for the former always indicate our power, the latter, on the other hand, show our infirmity and fragmentary knowledge.

3.

. . . Those desires and actions which are defined by man's power of reason are always good. The rest may be either good or bad.

4.

Thus in life it is before all things useful to perfect the understanding, or reason, as far as we can, and in this alone man's highest happiness or blessedness consists. Indeed blessedness is nothing else but the contentment of spirit, which arises from the intuitive knowledge of God. To perfect the understanding is nothing else but to understand God, God's attributes, and the actions which follow from the necessity of His nature. For a man, who is led by reason, the ultimate aim or highest desire, whereby he seeks to govern all his fellows, is that whereby he is brought to the adequate conception of himself and of all things within the scope of his intelligence.

5.

Without intelligence, there is no rational life; and things are only good, insofar as they aid man in his enjoyment of the intellectual life, which is defined by intelligence. Contrariwise, whatsoever things hinder man's perfecting of his reason, and capability to enjoy the rational life, are alone called evil.

6.

As all things of which man is the efficient cause are necessarily good, no evil can befall man except through external causes; that is, by virtue of man being a part of universal nature, whose laws human nature is compelled to obey, and with which to conform in almost infinite ways.

7.

It is impossible that man should not be a part of nature, or that he should not follow her general order. But if he be thrown among individuals whose nature is in harmony with his own, his power of action will thereby be aided and fostered, whereas, if he be thrown among such as are but very little in harmony with his nature, he will hardly be able to accommodate himself to them without undergoing a great change himself.

8.

Whatsoever in nature we deem to be evil, or to be capable of injuring our faculty for existing and enjoying the rational life, we may endeavor to remove in whatever way seems safest to us. On the other hand, whatever we deem to be good or useful for preserving our being, and enabling us to enjoy the rational life, we may appropriate to our use and employ as we think best. Everyone without exception may, by sovereign right of nature, do whatsoever he thinks will advance his own interest.

9.

Nothing can be in more harmony with the nature of any given thing than other individuals of the same species. Therefore (cf. IV: 7) for man in the preservation of his being and the enjoyment of the rational life, there is nothing more useful than a fellowman led by reason. Further, just as there is nothing more excellent than a man led by reason, no man can better display the power of his skill and disposition, than in so training men that they come at last to live under the dominion of their own reason.

10.

Insofar as men are influenced by envy or any kind of hatred, one towards another, they are at variance, and are therefore to be feared in proportion, as they are more powerful, than their fellows.

11.

Yet minds are not conquered by force, but by love and high-mindedness.

12.

It is before all things useful to men to associate in their ways of life, to bind themselves together with such bonds as they think most fitted to gather them all into unity, and generally to do whatsoever serves to strengthen friendship.

13.

But for this there is need of skill and watchfulness. Men are diverse; those who live under the guidance of reason are few; those who do not are generally envious and more prone to revenge than to sympathy. No small force of character is therefore required to take everyone as he is, and to restrain from imitating the emotions of others. But it is also true that those who carp at mankind, and are more skilled in railing at vice than in instilling virtue, and who break rather than strengthen men's dispositions, are hurtful both to themselves and others. Thus many from too great impatience of spirit, or from misguided religious zeal, have preferred to live among brutes rather than among men. They are like boys or youths, who cannot peaceably endure the chidings of their parents, so enlist as soldiers and choose the hardships of war and the despotic discipline in preference to the comforts of home and the admonitions of their father. They suffer any burden to be put upon them, so long as they may spite their parents.

14.

Although men are generally governed in everything by their own lusts, yet their association in common brings many more advantages than drawbacks. Therefore it is better to bear patiently the wrongs they may do us, and to strive to promote whatsoever serves to bring about harmony and friendship.

15.

Those things which beget harmony are associated with justice, equity, and honorable living. Men brook ill not only what is unjust or iniquitous, but also what is reckoned disgraceful, or that a man should slight the received customs of society. For winning love those qualities are especially necessary which have regard to religion and piety (cf. IV: 37 n1, n2; 46 n; 73 n).

16.

Harmony is often the result of fear, but such harmony is insecure. Further, fear arises from infirmity of spirit, and belongs not to the exercise of reason. The same is true of compassion, though this latter seems to bear a certain resemblance to piety.

17.

Men are also won over by liberality, especially such as have not the means to buy what is necessary to sustain life. However, to give aid to every poor man is far beyond the power and the advantage of any private person. For the riches of any private person are wholly inadequate to meet such a call. Similarly, an individual man's resources of character are too limited for him to be able to make all men his friends. Consequently providing for the poor is a duty which falls on the State as a whole, and provides a general advantage.

18.

In accepting favors and in returning gratitude our duty must be wholly different (cf. IV: 70 n, 71 n).

19.

Meretricious love, that is, the lust connected to physical beauty, and generally every sort of love which does not have freedom of soul as its cause, readily passes into hate. Or what is worse, it becomes a species of madness, and promotes discord rather than harmony (cf. III: 31 c).

20.

With regard to marriage, it is certain that it is in harmony with reason, if the desire for physical union be not engendered solely by physical beauty, but also by the desire to beget children and to train them up wisely. This is especially so if the love of both, to wit, the man and of the woman, is not driven by physical beauty only, but also by freedom of soul.

21.

Flattery begets harmony, but only by means of the vile offense of slavishness or treachery. None are more readily taken in by flattery than the proud, who wish to be first, but are not.

22.

There is in abasement a spurious appearance of piety and religion. Although abasement is the opposite to pride, yet he that abases himself is most akin to the proud (IV: 57 n).

23.

Shame also brings about harmony, but only in such matters as cannot be hid. Further, as shame is a species of pain, it does not involve the exercise of reason.

24.

The remaining painful emotions in our relations with men are directly opposed to justice, equity, honor, piety, and religion. Although indignation seems to bear a certain resemblance to equity, yet is life lawless, where every man may pass judgment on another's deeds, and vindicate his own or other men's rights.

25.

Correctness of conduct (*modestia*), that is, the desire of pleasing men which is determined by reason, is attributable to piety (as we said in IV: 37 n1). But, if it spring from emotion, it is ambition, the desire whereby men, under the false cloak of piety, generally stir up discords and seditions. For he who desires to aid his fellows either in word or in deed, so that they may together enjoy the highest good, he, I say, will before all things strive to win them over with love not to draw them into admiration, in order that a system may be called after his name, nor to give any cause for envy. Further, in his conversation he will shrink from talking of men's faults, and will be careful to speak but sparingly of human infirmity. He will instead dwell at length on human virtue or power, and the way whereby it may be perfected. Thus will men be stirred not by fear, nor by aversion, but only by the emotion of joy, to endeavor, so far as they can, to live in obedience to reason.

26.

Besides men, we know of nothing in nature in whose mind we may rejoice, and whom we can associate with ourselves in friendship or any sort of fellowship. Therefore, whatsoever there be in nature besides man, a regard for our advantage does not call on us to preserve, but to preserve or destroy according to its various capabilities, and to adapt to our use as best we may.

27.

The advantage which we derive from things external to us, besides the experience and knowledge which we acquire from observing them, and from recombining their elements in different forms, is principally the preservation of the body. From this point of view, those things are most useful which can so feed and nourish the body, that all its parts may rightly fulfill their functions. In proportion as the body is capable of being affected in a variety of ways, and of affecting external bodies in a great number of ways, so much the more is the mind capable of thinking (IV: 38, 39). For the due nourishment of the body, we must use many foods of diverse nature. For the human body is composed of very many parts of different nature, which stand in continual need of varied nourishment, so that the whole body may be equally capable of doing everything permitted by its own nature, and consequently that the mind also may be equally capable of forming many perceptions.

28.

For the task of providing these nourishments, the strength of each individual would hardly suffice if men did not lend one another mutual aid. But money has furnished us with a token for everything. Hence it is with the notion of money that the mind of the multitude is chiefly engrossed. It can hardly conceive any kind of pleasure which is not accompanied with the idea of money as cause.

29.

This result is the fault of those who seek money, not from poverty or to supply their necessary wants, but because they have learned the arts of gain and hope to bring themselves to great splendor. But they who know the true use of money, and who fix the measure of wealth solely with regard to their actual needs, live content with little.

30.

Because those things are good which assist the various parts of the body, and enable them to perform their functions; and because pleasure consists in an increase of, or aid to, man's power, insofar as he is composed of mind and body; it follows therefore that all those things which bring pleasure are good. But seeing that things do not work with the object of giving us pleasure, and that their power of action is not tempered to suit our advantage, and, lastly, that pleasure is generally referred to one part of the body more than to the other parts, most emotions of pleasure, and consequently the desires arising therefrom, may become excessive, unless restrained by reason and watchfulness. Moreover we may add that emotion leads us to pay most regard to what is agreeable in the present at the expense of the future; we cannot estimate what is future with emotions equally vivid (IV: 44 n, 60 n).

31.

Superstition seems to rate as good all that brings pain and as bad all that brings pleasure. However, none but the envious take delight in another's infirmity and trouble. For the greater the pleasure we experience, the greater is the perfection we experience, and consequently the more do we partake of the divine nature. No pleasure can ever be evil, which is regulated by a true regard for our advantage. But whoever is led by fear and does good only to avoid evil is not guided by reason.

32.

Human power is extremely limited, and is infinitely surpassed by the power of external causes. We have not, therefore, an absolute power of shaping to our use those things which are without us. Nevertheless, we shall bear with an equal mind all that happens to us in contravention to the claims of our own advantage, so long as we are conscious that we have done our duty, and that the power which we possess is not sufficient to enable us to protect ourselves completely we must remember that we are a part of universal nature and that we follow her order. If we have a clear and distinct understanding of this, that portion of our nature which is defined by intelligence, in other words the better part of ourselves, will assuredly acquiesce in what befalls us, and in such acquiescence will endeavor to persist. For, insofar as we are intelligent beings, we cannot desire anything save that which is necessary, nor yield absolute acquiescence to anything, save to that which is true. Insofar as we have a right understanding of these things, the endeavor of the better part of ourselves is in harmony with the order of nature as a whole.

. . . . .

[*The reasoning behind these conclusions is contained in Appendix B.*]

Part C

The Power of Reason
(Gaining Human Freedom)

A T LENGTH I pass to the remaining portion of my Ethics, where we are concerned with the way leading to freedom. I shall therefore treat of the power of the reason, showing how far the reason can control the emotions, and what is the nature of Mental Freedom or Blessedness. We shall then be able to see how much more powerful the wise man is than the ignorant. It is no part of my design to point out the method and means whereby the understanding may be perfected, nor to show the skill whereby the body may be so tended, as to be capable of the due performance of its functions. The latter question lies in the province of Medicine, the former in the province of Logic. Here, therefore, I repeat, I shall treat only of the power of the mind, or of reason; and I shall mainly show the extent and nature of its dominion over the emotions for their control and moderation.

That we do not possess absolute dominion over the emotions, I have already shown. But how potent is the wise man, and how much he surpasses the ignorant man, who is driven only by his lusts. For the ignorant man is not only distracted in various ways by external causes without ever gaining the true acquiescence of his spirit, but moreover lives, as it were unwitting of himself, and of God, and of things, and as soon as he ceases to suffer, ceases also to be.

By contrast the wise man, insofar as he is regarded as such, is scarcely at all disturbed in spirit, but, being conscious of himself, and of God, and of things, by a certain eternal necessity, never ceases to be, but always possesses true acquiescence of his spirit.

If the way which I have pointed out as leading to this result seems exceedingly hard, it may nevertheless be discovered. It must be hard, since it is so seldom found. How would it be possible, if salvation were ready to our hand, and could without great labor be found, that it should be by almost all men neglected? All things excellent are as difficult as they are rare.

It remains to point out the advantages of a knowledge of this doctrine as bearing on conduct, which may be easily gathered from what has been said. The doctrine is good, because it teaches us to act solely according to the decree of God, and to be partakers in the Divine nature, and so much the more, as we perform more perfect actions and more and more understand God. Such a doctrine not only completely tranquillizes our spirit, but also shows us where our highest happiness or blessedness is, namely, solely in the knowledge of God, whereby we are led to act only as love and piety shall bid us. We may thus clearly understand how far astray from a true estimate of virtue are those who expect to be decorated by God with high rewards for their virtue, and their best actions, as for having endured the direst slavery. Virtue and the service of God is in itself happiness and perfect freedom.

Our doctrine also teaches us how we ought to conduct ourselves with respect to the gifts of fortune or matters which are not in our own power, and do not follow from our nature. For it shows us that we should await and endure fortune's smiles or frowns with an equal mind, seeing that all things follow from the eternal decree of God by the same necessity, as it follows from the essence of a triangle, where the three angles are always equal to two right angles.

This doctrine raises social life, inasmuch as it teaches us to hate no man, neither to despise, to deride, to envy, nor to be angry with any. Further, it tells us that each should be content with his own and helpful to his neighbor, not from any womanish pity, favor, or superstition, but solely by the guidance of reason, according as the time and occasion demand.

Lastly, this doctrine confers no small advantage on the commonwealth, for it teaches how citizens should be governed and led, not so as to become slaves, but so that they may freely do whatsoever things are best.

. . . . .

[*The reasoning behind these conclusions is contained in Appendix C.*]

Appendix A
God

Part I: Concerning God

PROP. 11:

GOD, OR SUBSTANCE, consisting of infinite attributes, of which each expresses eternal and infinite essentiality, necessarily exists.

PROOF: If this be denied, conceive, if possible, that God does not exist: then his essence does not involve existence. But this (by I: 7) is absurd. Therefore God necessarily exists.

ANOTHER PROOF: Of everything whatsoever a cause or reason must be assigned, either for its existence, or for its nonexistence—e.g. if a triangle exists, a reason or cause must be granted for its existence; if, on the contrary, it does not exist, a cause must also be granted, which prevents it from existing, or annuls its existence. This reason or cause must either be contained in the nature of the thing in question, or be external to it. For instance, the reason for the nonexistence of a square circle is indicated in its nature, namely, because it would involve a contradiction. On the other hand, the existence of substance follows also solely from its nature, inasmuch as its nature involves existence. (See I: 7.)

But the reason for the existence of a triangle or a circle does not follow from the nature of those figures, but from the order of universal nature in extension. From the latter it must follow, either that a triangle necessarily exists, or that it is impossible that it should exist. So much is self-evident. It follows therefrom that a thing necessarily exists if no cause or reason be granted which prevents its existence.

If, then, no cause or reason can be given, which prevents the existence of God, or which destroys his existence, we must certainly conclude that he necessarily does exist. If such a reason or cause should be given, it must either be drawn from the very nature of God, or be external to him—that is, drawn from another substance of another nature. For if it was of the same nature, God, by that very fact, would be admitted to exist. But substance of another nature could have nothing in common with God (by I: 2), and therefore would be unable either to cause or to destroy his existence.

As, then, a reason or cause which would annul the divine existence cannot be drawn from anything external to the divine nature, such cause must perforce, if God does not exist, be drawn from God's own nature, which would involve a contradiction. To make such an affirmation about a being absolutely infinite and supremely perfect, is absurd; therefore, neither in the nature of God, nor externally to his nature, can a cause or reason be assigned which would annul his existence. Therefore, God necessarily exists. QED.*

ANOTHER PROOF: The potentiality of nonexistence is a negation of power, and contrariwise the potentiality of existence is a power, as is obvious. If, then, that which necessarily exists is nothing but finite beings, such finite beings are more powerful than a being absolutely infinite, which is obviously absurd; therefore, either nothing exists, or else a being absolutely infinite necessarily exists also. Now we exist either in ourselves, or in something else which necessarily exists (see I: ax1, ax7). Therefore a being absolutely infinite—in other words, God (I: def6)—necessarily exists. QED.

---

* QED stands for the Latin phrase *quod erat demonstrandum*, "that which was to be demonstrated." It is traditionally placed at the end of a philosophical argument when what was stated at the beginning of the proposition has been exactly restated as a conclusion, as if to say, "There, I've proved it."

NOTE: In this last proof, I have purposely shown God's existence *a posteriori*, so that the proof might be more easily followed, not because, from the same premises, God's existence does not follow *a priori*. For, as the potentiality of existence is a power, it follows that, in proportion as reality increases in the nature of a thing, so also will it increase its strength for existence. Therefore a being absolutely infinite, such as God, has from himself an absolutely infinite power of existence, and hence he does absolutely exist. Perhaps there will be many who will be unable to see the force of this proof, inasmuch as they are accustomed only to consider those things which flow from external causes. Of such things, they see that those which quickly come to pass—that is, quickly come into existence—quickly also disappear; whereas they regard as more difficult of accomplishment—that is, not so easily brought into existence—those things which they conceive as more complicated.

However, to do away with this misconception, I need not here show the measure of truth in the proverb, "What comes quickly, goes quickly," nor discuss whether, from the point of view of universal nature, all things are equally easy, or otherwise: I need only remark, that I am not here speaking of things, which come to pass through causes external to themselves, but only of substances which (by I: 6) cannot be produced by any external cause. Things which are produced by external causes, whether they consist of many parts or few, owe whatsoever perfection or reality they possess solely to the efficacy of their external cause, and therefore their existence arises solely from the perfection of their external cause, not from their own. Contrariwise, whatsoever perfection is possessed by substance is due to no external cause: wherefore the existence of substance must arise solely from its own nature, which is nothing else but its essence. Thus, the perfection of a thing does not annul its existence, but, on the contrary, asserts it. Imperfection, on the other hand, does annul it; therefore we cannot be more certain of the existence of anything than of the existence of a being absolutely infinite or perfect—that is, of God. For inasmuch as his essence excludes all imperfection, and involves absolute perfection, all cause for doubt concerning his existence is done away, and the utmost certainty on the question is given. This, I think, will be evident to every moderately attentive reader. . . .

PROP. 15:

Whatsoever is, is in God, and without God nothing can be, or be conceived. . . .

PROP. 16:

From the necessity of the divine nature must follow an infinite number of things in infinite ways—that is, all things which can fall within the sphere of infinite intellect.

PROOF: This proposition will be clear to everyone, who remembers that from the given definition of any thing the intellect infers several properties, which really necessarily follow therefrom (that is, from the actual essence of the thing defined); and it infers more properties in proportion as the definition of the thing expresses more reality, that is, in proportion as the essence of the thing defined involves more reality. Now, as the divine nature has absolutely infinite attributes (by I: def6), of which each expresses infinite essence after its kind, it follows that from the necessity of its nature an infinite number of things (that is, everything which can fall within the sphere of an infinite intellect) must necessarily follow. QED.

COROLLARY 1: Hence it follows, that God is the efficient cause of all that can fall within the sphere of an infinite intellect.

COROLLARY 2: It also follows that God is a cause in himself, and not through an accident of his nature. . . .

COROLLARY 3: It follows, thirdly, that God is the absolutely first cause. . . .

Appendix B
Mind and Emotion

Part II: Of the Nature and Origin of the Mind

NOTE: THE MULTITUDE understand by the power of God the free will of God, and the right over all things that exist, which are accordingly generally considered as contingent. For it is said that God has the power to destroy all things, and to reduce them to nothing. Further, the power of God is very often likened to the power of kings. But this doctrine we have refuted (I: 32 c1, c2), and we have shown (I: 16) that God acts by the same necessity, as that by which he understands himself; in other words, as it follows from the necessity of the divine nature (as all admit), that God understands himself, so also does it follow by the same necessity, that God performs infinite acts in infinite ways. We further showed (I: 34), that God's power is identical with God's essence in action; therefore it is as impossible for us to conceive God as not acting, as to conceive him as nonexistent. If we might pursue the subject further, I could point out that the power which is commonly attributed to God is not only human (as showing that God is conceived by the multitude as a man, or in the likeness of a man), but involves a negation of power.

Part III: On the Origin and Nature of the Emotions

Most writers on the emotions and on human conduct seem to be treating rather of matters outside nature than of natural phenomena following nature's general laws. They appear to conceive man to be situated in nature as a kingdom within a kingdom: for they believe that he disturbs rather than follows nature's order, that he has absolute control over his actions, and that he is determined solely by himself. They attribute human infirmities and fickleness, not to the power of nature in general, but to some mysterious flaw in the nature of man, which accordingly they bemoan, deride, despise, or, as usually happens, abuse: he, who succeeds in hitting off the weakness of the human mind more eloquently or more acutely than his fellows, is looked upon as a seer. Still there has been no lack of very excellent men (to whose toil and industry I confess myself much indebted), who have written many noteworthy things concerning the right way of life, and have given much sage advice to mankind. But no one, so far as I know, has defined the nature and strength of the emotions, and the power of the mind against them for their restraint.

I do not forget, that the illustrious Descartes, though he believed that the mind has absolute power over its actions, strove to explain human emotions by their primary causes, and, at the same time, to point out a way, by which the mind might attain to absolute dominion over them. However, in my opinion, he accomplishes nothing beyond a display of the acuteness of his own great intellect, as I will show in the proper place. For the present I wish to revert to those, who would rather abuse or deride human emotions than understand them. Such persons will doubtless think it strange that I should attempt to treat of human vice and folly logically, and should wish to set forth with rigid reasoning those matters which they cry out against as repugnant to reason, frivolous, absurd, and dreadful. However, such is my plan.

Nothing comes to pass in nature, which can be set down to a flaw therein; for nature is always the same, and everywhere one and the same in her efficacy and power of action; that is, nature's laws and ordinances, whereby all things come to pass and change from one form to another, are everywhere and always the same; so that there should be one and the same method of understanding the nature of all things whatsoever, namely, through nature's universal laws and rules. Thus the passions of hatred, anger, envy, and so on, considered in themselves, follow from this same necessity and efficacy of nature; they answer to certain definite causes, through which they are understood, and possess certain properties as worthy of being known as the properties of anything else, whereof the contemplation in itself affords us delight. I shall, therefore, treat of the nature and strength of the emotions according to the same method, as I employed heretofore in my investigations concerning God and the mind. I shall consider human actions and desires in exactly the same geometric manner, as though I were concerned with lines, planes, and solids. . . .

NOTE: This endeavor, when referred solely to the mind, is called *will*, when referred to the mind and body in conjunction it is called *appetite*; it is, in fact, nothing else but man's essence, from the nature of which necessarily follow all those results which tend to its preservation; and which man has thus been determined to perform.

Further, between appetite and desire there is no difference, except that the term desire is generally applied to men, insofar as they are conscious of their appetite, and may accordingly be thus defined: *Desire is appetite with consciousness thereof.* It is thus plain from what has been said, that in no case do we strive for, wish for, long for, or desire anything, because we deem it to be good, but on the other hand we deem a thing to be good, because we strive for it, wish for it, long for it, or desire it. . . .

NOTE: Thus we see that the mind can undergo many changes, and can pass sometimes to a state of greater perfection, sometimes to a state of lesser perfection. These passive states of transition explain to us the emotions of pleasure and pain. By *pleasure* therefore in the following propositions I shall signify *a passive state wherein the mind passes to a greater perfection.* By *pain* I shall signify *a passive state wherein the mind passes to a lesser perfection.* Further, the emotion of pleasure in reference to the body and mind together I shall call *stimulation* (*titillatio*) or *merriment* (*hilaritas*), the emotion of pain in the same relation I shall call *suffering* or *melancholy.* But we must bear in mind that stimulation and suffering are attributed to man when one part of his nature is more affected than the rest, merriment and melancholy when all parts are alike affected.

What I mean by desire I have explained in III: 9 n of this part; beyond these three I recognize no other primary emotion; I will show as I proceed that all other emotions arise from these three: pleasure/stimulation, pain/melancholy, and desire. . . .

NOTE: From what has been said we may clearly understand the nature of Love and Hate. *Love* is nothing else but *pleasure accompanied by the idea of an external cause*; *Hate* is nothing else but *pain accompanied by the idea of an external cause*. We further see that he who loves necessarily endeavors to have, and to keep present to him, the object of his love; while he who hates endeavors to remove and destroy the object of his hatred. But I will treat of these matters at more length hereafter. . . .

NOTE 2: From what has just been said, we understand what is meant by the terms Hope, Fear, Confidence, Despair, Joy, and Disappointment. *Hope* is nothing else but *an inconstant pleasure, arising from the image of something future or past, whereof we do not yet know the issue. Fear*, on the other hand, is *an inconstant pain also arising from the image of something concerning which we are in doubt.* If the element of doubt be removed from these emotions, hope becomes *Confidence* and fear becomes *Despair.* In other words, *Pleasure or Pain arising from the image of something concerning which we have hoped or feared.* Again, *Joy* is *Pleasure arising from the image of something past whereof we doubted the issue. Disappointment is the Pain opposed to Joy.* . . .

NOTE: III: 21 explains to us the nature of *Pity*, which we may define as *pain arising from another's hurt*. What term we can use for pleasure arising from another's gain, I know not.

We will call the *love towards him who confers a benefit on another, Approval*; and the *hatred towards him who injures another*, we will call *Indignation*. We must further remark, that we not only feel pity for a thing which we have loved (as shown in III: 21), but also for a thing which we have hitherto regarded without emotion, provided that we deem that it resembles ourselves (as I will show presently). Thus, we bestow approval on one who has benefited anything resembling ourselves, and, contrariwise, are indignant with him who has done it an injury. . . .

NOTE: Thus we see that it may readily happen, that a man may easily think too highly of himself, or a loved object, and, contrariwise, too meanly of a hated object. This feeling is called *pride*, in reference to the man who thinks too highly of himself, and is a species of madness, wherein a man dreams with his eyes open, thinking that he can accomplish all things that fall within the scope of his conception, and thereupon accounting them real, and exulting in them, so long as he is unable to conceive anything which excludes their existence, and determines his own power of action. *Pride*, therefore, is *pleasure springing from a man thinking too highly of himself*. Again, the *pleasure which arises from a man thinking too highly of another* is called *over-esteem*. Whereas the *pleasure which arises from thinking too little of a man* is called *disdain*. . . .

NOTE: This imitation of emotions, when it is referred to pain, is called *compassion* (cf. III: 22 n); when it is referred to desire, it is called *emulation*, which is nothing else but *the desire of anything, engendered in us by the fact that we conceive that others have the like desire*. . . .

NOTE: This will or appetite for doing good, which arises from pity of the thing whereon we would confer a benefit, is called *benevolence*, and is nothing else but *desire arising from compassion*. Concerning love or hate towards him who has done good or harm to something, which we conceive to be like ourselves, see III: 22 n. . . .

NOTE: This endeavor to do a thing or leave it undone, solely in order to please men, we call *ambition*, especially when we so eagerly endeavor to please the vulgar, that we do or omit certain things to our own or another's hurt: in other cases it is generally called *kindliness*. Furthermore I give the name of *praise* to the *pleasure with which we conceive the action of another, whereby he has endeavored to please us*; but of *blame* to the *pain wherewith we feel aversion to his action*. . . .

NOTE: As love (III: 13) is pleasure accompanied by the idea of an external cause, and hatred is pain accompanied by the idea of an external cause, the pleasure and pain in question will be a species of love and hatred. But, as the terms love and hatred are used in reference to external objects, we will employ other names for the emotions now under discussion: pleasure accompanied by the idea of an external cause we will style *Honor*, and the emotion contrary thereto we will style *Shame*. I mean in such cases as where pleasure or pain arises from a man's belief, that he is being praised or blamed: otherwise pleasure accompanied by the idea of an external cause is called *self-complacency*, and its contrary pain is called *repentance*. Again, as it may happen (II: 17 c) that the pleasure, wherewith a man conceives that he affects others, may exist solely in his own imagination, and as (III: 25) everyone endeavors to conceive concerning himself that which he conceives will affect him with pleasure, it may easily come to pass that a vain man may be proud and may imagine that he is pleasing to all, when in reality he may be an annoyance to all. . . .

NOTE: This endeavor to bring it about, that our own likes and dislikes should meet with universal approval, is really ambition (see III: 29 n); wherefore we see that everyone by nature desires (*appetere*) that the rest of mankind should live according to his own individual disposition: when such a desire is equally present in all, everyone stands in everyone else's way, and in wishing to be loved or praised by all, all become mutually hateful. . . .

NOTE: This hatred towards an object of love joined with envy is called *Jealousy*, which accordingly is nothing else but a wavering of the disposition arising from combined love and hatred, accompanied by the idea of some rival who is envied. Further, this hatred towards the object of love will be greater, in proportion to the pleasure which the jealous man had been wont to derive from the reciprocated love of the said object; and also in proportion to the feelings he had previously entertained towards his rival. If he had hated him, he will forthwith hate the object of his love, because he conceives it is pleasurably affected by one whom he himself hates: and also because he is compelled to associate the image of his loved one with the image of him whom he hates. This condition generally comes into play in the case of love for a woman: for he who thinks that a woman whom he loves prostitutes herself to another, will feel pain, not only because his own desire is restrained, but also because, being compelled to associate the image of her he loves with the parts of shame and the excreta of another, he therefore shrinks from her.

We must add, that a jealous man is not greeted by his beloved with the same joyful countenance as before, and this also gives him pain as a lover, as I will now show. . . .

NOTE: This pain, insofar as it has reference to the absence of the object of love, is called *Regret*. . . .

Lastly, since hatred and love are themselves emotions of pain and pleasure, it follows in like manner that the endeavor, appetite, or desire, which arises through hatred or love, will be greater in proportion to the hatred or love. QED.

PROP. 38:

If a man has begun to hate an object of his love, so that love is thoroughly destroyed, he will, causes being equal, regard it with more hatred than if he had never loved it, and his hatred will be in proportion to the strength of his former love.

PROOF: If a man begins to hate that which he had loved, more of his appetites are put under restraint than if he had never loved it. For love is a pleasure (III: 13 n) which a man endeavors as far as he can to render permanent (III: 28); he does so by regarding the object of his love as present, and by affecting it as far as he can pleasurably; this endeavor is greater in proportion as the love is greater, and so also is the endeavor to bring about that the beloved should return his affection (III: 33). Now these endeavors are constrained by hatred towards the object of love (III: 13 c, 23); wherefore the lover (III: 11 n) will for this cause also be affected with pain, the more so in proportion as his love has been greater; that is, in addition to the pain caused by hatred, there is a pain caused by the fact that he has loved the object; wherefore the lover will regard the beloved with greater pain, or in other words, will hate it more than if he had never loved it, and with the more intensity in proportion as his former love was greater. QED....

NOTE: By *good* I here mean every kind of pleasure and all that conduces thereto, especially that which satisfies our longings, whatsoever they may be. By *evil*, I mean every kind of pain, especially that which frustrates our longings. For I have shown (III: 9 n) that we in no case desire a thing because we deem it good, but, contrariwise, we deem a thing good because we desire it: consequently we deem evil that which we shrink from; everyone, therefore, according to his particular emotions, judges or estimates what is good, what is bad, what is better, what is worse; lastly, what is best, and what is worst. Thus a miser thinks that abundance of money is the best, and want of money the worst; an ambitious man desires nothing so much as glory, and fears nothing so much as shame. To an envious man nothing is more delightful than another's misfortune, and nothing more painful than another's success. So every man, according to his emotions, judges a thing to be good or bad, useful or useless. The emotion, which induces a man to turn from that which he wishes, or to wish for that which he turns from, is called *timidity*, which may accordingly be defined as *the fear whereby* *a man is induced to avoid an evil which he regards as future by encountering a lesser evil* (III: 28). But if the evil which he fears be shame, timidity becomes *bashfulness.* Lastly, if the desire to avoid a future evil be checked by the fear of another evil, so that the man knows not which to choose, fear becomes *consternation*, especially if both the evils feared be very great. . . .

NOTE: If hatred be the prevailing emotion, he will endeavor to injure him who loves him; this emotion is called cruelty, especially if the victim be believed to have given no ordinary cause for hatred. . . .

An example of the deductive, geometric method applied to the study of human beings:

PROP. 43:

Hatred is increased by being reciprocated, and can on the other hand be destroyed by love.

PROOF: He who conceives, that an object of his hate hates him in return, will thereupon feel a new hatred, while the former hatred (by hypothesis) still remains (III: 40). But if, on the other hand, he conceives that the object of hate loves him, he will to this extent (III: 38) regard himself with pleasure, and (III: 29) will endeavor to please the cause of his emotion. In other words, he will endeavor not to hate him (III: 41), and not to affect him painfully; this endeavor (III: 37) will be greater or less in proportion to the emotion from which it arises.

Therefore, if it be greater than that which arises from hatred, and through which the man endeavors to affect painfully the thing which he hates, it will get the better of it and banish the hatred from his mind. QED.

PROP. 44:

Hatred which is completely vanquished by love passes into love: and love is thereupon greater than if hatred had not preceded it.

PROOF: The proof proceeds in the same way as III: 38: for he who begins to love a thing, which he was wont to hate or regard with pain, from the very fact of loving feels pleasure. To this pleasure involved in love is added the pleasure arising from aid given to the endeavor to remove the pain involved in hatred (III: 37), accompanied by the idea of the former object of hatred as cause.

NOTE: Though this be so, no one will endeavor to hate anything, or to be affected with pain, for the sake of enjoying this greater pleasure; that is, no one will desire that he should be injured, in the hope of recovering from the injury, nor long to be ill for the sake of getting well. For everyone will always endeavor to persist in his being, and to ward off pain as far as he can. If the contrary is conceivable, namely, that a man should desire to hate someone, in order that he might love him the more thereafter, he will always desire to hate him. For the strength of the love is in proportion to the strength of the hatred, wherefore the man would desire, that the hatred be continually increased more and more, and, for a similar reason, he would desire to become more and more ill, in order that he might take a greater pleasure in being restored to health: in such a case he would always endeavor to be ill, which (III: 6) is absurd. . . .

Another example:

PROP. 46:

If a man has been affected pleasurably or painfully by anyone, of a class or nation different from his own, and if the pleasure or pain has been accompanied by the idea of the said stranger as cause, under the general category of the class or nation: the man will feel love or hatred, not only to the individual stranger, but also to the whole class or nation whereto he belongs.

PROOF: This is evident from III: 16.

PROP. 47:

Joy arising from the fact, that anything we hate is destroyed, or suffers other injury, is never unaccompanied by a certain pain in us.

PROOF: This is evident from III: 27. For insofar as we conceive a thing similar to ourselves to be affected with pain, we ourselves feel pain.

NOTE: This proposition can also be proved from II: 17 c. Whenever we remember anything, even if it does not actually exist, we regard it only as present, and the body is affected in the same manner; wherefore, insofar as the remembrance of the thing is strong, a man is determined to regard it with pain; this determination, while the image of the thing in question lasts, is indeed checked by the remembrance of other things excluding the existence of the aforesaid thing, but is not destroyed: hence, a man only feels pleasure insofar as the said determination is checked; for this reason the joy arising from the injury done to what we hate is repeated, every time we remember that object of hatred. For, as we have said, when the image of the thing in question is aroused, inasmuch as it involves the thing's existence, it determines the man to regard the thing with the same pain as he was wont to do, when it actually did exist. However, since he has joined to the image of the thing other images, which exclude its existence, this determination to pain is forthwith checked, and the man rejoices afresh as often as the repetition takes place. This is the cause of men's pleasure in recalling past evils, and delight in narrating dangers from which they have escaped. For when men conceive a danger, they conceive it as still future, and are determined to fear it; this determination is checked afresh by the idea of freedom, which became associated with the idea of the danger when they escaped therefrom: this renders them secure afresh; therefore they rejoice afresh. . . .

NOTE: We thus see that it is possible, that what one man loves another may hate, and that what one man fears another may not fear; or, again, that one and the same man may love what he once hated, or may be bold where he once was timid, and so on. Again, as everyone judges according to his emotions what is good, what bad, what better, and what worse (III: 39 n), it follows that men's judgments may vary no less than their emotions, hence when we compare some with others, we distinguish them solely by the diversity of their emotions, and style some intrepid, others timid, others by some other epithet. For instance, I shall call a man *intrepid*, if he despises an evil which I am accustomed to fear; if I further take into consideration, that, in his desire to injure his enemies and to benefit those whom he loves, he is not restrained by the fear of an evil which is sufficient to restrain me, I shall call him *daring*. Again, a man will appear *timid* to me, if he fears an evil which I am accustomed to despise; and if I further take into consideration that his desire is restrained by the fear of an evil, which is not sufficient to restrain me, I shall say that he is *cowardly*; and in like manner will everyone pass judgment.

Lastly, from this inconstancy in the nature of human judgment, inasmuch as a man often judges of things solely by his emotions, and inasmuch as the things which he believes cause pleasure or pain, and therefore endeavors to promote or prevent, are often purely imaginary, not to speak of the uncertainty of things alluded to in III: 28; we may readily conceive that a man may be at one time affected with pleasure, and at another with pain, accompanied by the idea of himself as cause. Thus we can easily understand what are *Repentance* and *Self-complacency*, *Repentance is pain, accompanied by the idea of one's self as cause*; *Self-complacency is pleasure accompanied by the idea of one's self as cause*, and these emotions are most intense because men believe themselves to be free (III: 49). . . .

NOTE: . . . Pain, accompanied by the idea of our own weakness, is called *humility*; the pleasure, which springs from the contemplation of ourselves, is called *self-love* or *self-complacency*. And inasmuch as this feeling is renewed as often as a man contemplates his own virtues, or his own power of activity, it follows that everyone is fond of narrating his own exploits, and displaying the force both of his body and mind, and also that, for this reason, men are troublesome one to another. Again, it follows that men are naturally envious (III: 24 n, 32 n), rejoicing in the shortcomings of their equals, and feeling pain at their virtues. For whenever a man conceives his own actions, he is affected with pleasure (III: 53), in proportion as his actions display more perfection, and he conceives them more distinctly—that is (II: 40 n), in proportion as he can distinguish them from others, and regard them as something special. Therefore, a man will take most pleasure in contemplating himself, when he contemplates some quality which he denies to others. But, if that which he affirms of himself be attributable to the idea of man or animals in general, he will not be so greatly pleased: he will, on the contrary, feel pain, if he conceives that his own actions fall short when compared with those of others. This pain (III: 28) he will endeavor to remove, by putting a wrong construction on the actions of his equals, or by, as far as he can, embellishing his own.

It is thus apparent that men are naturally prone to hatred and envy, which latter is fostered by their education. For parents are accustomed to incite their children to virtue solely by the spur of honor and envy. But, perhaps, some will scruple to assent to what I have said, because we not seldom admire men's virtues, and venerate their possessors. In order to remove such doubts, I append the following corollary....

3rd example on "geometric" method applied to study of people:

Prop. 56:

There are as many kinds of pleasure, of pain, of desire, and of every emotion compounded of these, such as vacillations of spirit, or derived from these, such as love, hatred, hope, fear, etc., as there are kinds of objects whereby we are affected.

PROOF: Pleasure and pain, and consequently the emotions compounded thereof, or derived therefrom, are passions, or passive states (III: 11 n); now we are necessarily passive (III: 1), insofar as we have inadequate ideas; and only insofar as we have such ideas are we passive (III: 3); that is, we are only necessarily passive (II: 40 n), insofar as we conceive, or (II: 17 and n) insofar as we are affected by an emotion, which involves the nature of our own body, and the nature of an external body. Wherefore the nature of every passive state must necessarily be so explained, that the nature of the object whereby we are affected be expressed. Namely, the pleasure, which arises from, say, the object a, involves the nature of that object a, and the pleasure, which arises from the object b, involves the nature of the object b; wherefore these two pleasurable emotions are by nature different, inasmuch as the causes whence they arise are by nature different. So again the emotion of pain, which arises from one object, is by nature different from the pain arising from another object, and, similarly, in the case of love, hatred, hope, fear, vacillation, etc.

Thus, there are necessarily as many kinds of pleasure, pain, love, hatred, etc., as there are kinds of objects whereby we are affected. Now desire is each man's essence or nature, insofar as it is conceived as determined to a particular action by any given modification of itself (III: 9 n); therefore, according as a man is affected through external causes by this or that kind of pleasure, pain, love, hatred, etc., in other words, according as his nature is disposed in this or that manner, so will his desire be of one kind or another, and the nature of one desire must necessarily differ from the nature of another desire, as widely as the cmotions differ, wherefrom each desire arose. Thus there are as many kinds of desire, as there are kinds of pleasure, pain, love, etc., consequently (by what has been shown) there are as many kinds of desire, as there are kinds of objects whereby we are affected. QED.

NOTE: Among the kinds of emotions, which, by the last proposition, must be very numerous, the chief are *luxury*, *drunkenness*, *lust, avarice*, and *ambition*, being merely species of love or desire, displaying the nature of those emotions in a manner varying according to the object, with which they are concerned. For by luxury, drunkenness, lust, avarice, ambition, etc., we simply mean the immoderate love of feasting, drinking, venery, riches, and fame. Furthermore, these emotions, insofar as we distinguish them from others merely by the objects wherewith they are concerned, have no contraries. For *temperance*, *sobriety*, and *chastity*, which we are wont to oppose to luxury, drunkenness, and lust, are not emotions or passive states, but indicate a power of the mind which moderates the last-named emotions. However, I cannot here explain the remaining kinds of emotions (seeing that they are as numerous as the kinds of objects), nor, if I could, would it be necessary. It is sufficient for our purpose, namely, to determine the strength of the emotions, and the mind's power over them, to have a general definition of each emotion. It is sufficient, I repeat, to understand the general properties of the emotions and the mind, to enable us to determine the quality and extent of the mind's power in moderating and checking the emotions. Thus, though there is a great difference between various emotions of love, hatred, or desire, for instance between love felt towards children, and love felt towards a wife, there is no need for us to take cognizance of such differences, or to track out further the nature and origin of the emotions. . . .

NOTE: Hence it follows, that the emotions of the animals which are called irrational (for after learning the origin of mind we cannot doubt that brutes feel) only differ from man's emotions, to the extent that brute nature differs from human nature. Horse and man are alike carried away by the desire of procreation; but the desire of the former is equine, the desire of the latter is human. So also the lusts and appetites of insects, fishes, and birds must needs vary according to the several natures. Thus, although each individual lives content and rejoices in that nature belonging to him wherein he has his being, yet the life, wherein each is content and rejoices, is nothing else but the idea, or soul, of the said individual, and hence the joy of one only differs in nature from the joy of another, to the extent that the essence of one differs from the essence of another. Lastly, it follows from the foregoing proposition, that there is no small difference between the joy which actuates, say, a drunkard, and the joy possessed by a philosopher, as I just mention here by the way. Thus far I have treated of the emotions attributable to man, insofar as he is passive. It remains to add a few words on those attributable to him insofar as he is active. . . .

I think I have thus explained, and displayed through their primary causes the principal emotions and vacillations of spirit, which arise from the combination of the three primary emotions, to wit, desire, pleasure, and pain. It is evident from what I have said, that we are in many ways driven about by external causes, and that like waves of the sea driven by contrary winds we toss to and fro unwitting of the issue and of our fate. But I have said that I have only set forth the chief conflicting emotions not all that might be given. For, by proceeding in the same way as above, we can easily show that love is united to repentance, scorn, shame, etc. I think everyone will agree from what has been said, that the emotions may be compounded one with another in so many ways, and so many variations may arise therefrom, as to exceed all possibility of computation.

For my purpose, however, it is enough to have enumerated the most important; to reckon up the rest which I have omitted would be more curious than profitable. It remains to remark concerning love, that it very often happens that while we are enjoying a thing which we longed for, the body, from the act of enjoyment, acquires a new disposition, whereby it is determined in another way, other images of things are aroused in it, and the mind begins to conceive and desire something fresh. For example, when we conceive something which generally delights us with its flavor, we desire to enjoy, that is, to eat it. But whilst we are thus enjoying it, the stomach is filled and the body is otherwise disposed. If, therefore, when the body is thus otherwise disposed, the image of the food which is present be stimulated, and consequently the endeavor or desire to eat it be stimulated also, the new disposition of the body will feel repugnance to the desire or attempt, and consequently the presence of the food which we formerly longed for will become odious. This revulsion of feeling is called *satiety* or weariness. For the rest, I have neglected the outward modifications of the body observable in emotions, such, for instance, as trembling, pallor, sobbing, laughter, etc., for these are attributable to the body only, without any reference to the mind. . . .

Part IV: Of Human Bondage, or the Strength of the Emotions

Human infirmity in moderating and checking the emotions I name bondage: for, when a man is a prey to his emotions, he is not his own master, but lies at the mercy of fortune; so much so, that he is often compelled, while seeing that which is better for him, to follow that which is worse. Why this is so, and what is good or evil in the emotions, I propose to show in this part of my treatise. But, before I begin, it would be well to make a few prefatory observations on perfection and imperfection, good and evil. . . .

Now we showed in Part I, that Nature does not work with an end in view. For the eternal and infinite Being, which we call God or Nature, acts by the same necessity as that whereby it exists. For we have shown, that by the same necessity of its nature, whereby it exists, it likewise works (I: 16). The reason or cause why God or Nature exists, and the reason why he acts, are one and the same. Therefore, as he does not exist for the sake of an end, so neither does he act for the sake of an end; of his existence and of his action there is neither origin nor end. Wherefore, a cause which is called final is nothing else but human desire, insofar as it is considered as the origin or cause of anything. For example, when we say that to be inhabited is the final cause of this or that house, we mean nothing more than that a man, conceiving the conveniences of household life, had a desire to build a house. Wherefore, the being inhabited, insofar as it is regarded as a final cause, is nothing else but this particular desire, which is really the efficient cause; it is regarded as the primary cause, because men are generally ignorant of the causes of their desires. They are, as I have often said already, conscious of their own actions and appetites, but ignorant of the causes whereby they are determined to any particular desire.

Therefore, the common saying that Nature sometimes falls short, or blunders, and produces things which are imperfect, I set down among the glosses treated of in Part I. Perfection and imperfection, then, are in reality merely modes of thinking, or notions which we form from a comparison among one another of individuals of the same species; hence I said above (II: def6), that by reality and perfection I mean the same thing. For we are wont to refer all the individual things in nature to one genus, which is called the highest genus, namely, to the category of Being, whereto absolutely all individuals in nature belong. Thus, insofar as we refer the individuals in nature to this category, and comparing them one with another, find that some possess more of being or reality than others, we, to this extent, say that some are more perfect than others. Again, insofar as we attribute to them anything implying negation—as term, end, infirmity, etc.—we, to this extent, call them imperfect, because they do not affect our mind so much as the things which we call perfect, not because they have any intrinsic deficiency, or because Nature has blundered. For nothing lies within the scope of a thing's nature, save that which follows from the necessity of the nature of its efficient cause, and whatsoever follows from the necessity of the nature of its efficient cause necessarily comes to pass.

As for the terms *good* and *bad*, they indicate no positive quality in things regarded in themselves, but are merely modes of thinking, or notions which we form from the comparison of things one with another. Thus one and the same thing can be at the same time good, bad, and indifferent. For instance, music is good for him that is melancholy, bad for him that mourns; for him that is deaf, it is neither good nor bad.

Nevertheless, though this be so, the terms should still be retained. For, inasmuch as we desire to form an idea of man as a type of human nature which we may hold in view, it will be useful for us to retain the terms in question, in the sense I have indicated.

In what follows, then, I shall mean by "good" that which we certainly know to be a means of approaching more nearly to the type of human nature, which we have set before ourselves; by "bad," that which we certainly know to be a hindrance to us in approaching the said type. Again, we shall say that men are more perfect, or more imperfect, in proportion as they approach more or less nearly to the said type. For it must be specially remarked that, when I say that a man passes from a lesser to a greater perfection, or *vice versa*, I do not mean that he is changed from one essence or reality to another; for instance, a horse would be as completely destroyed by being changed into a man, as by being changed into an insect. What I mean is, that we conceive the thing's power of action, insofar as this is understood by its nature, to be increased or diminished. Lastly, by perfection in general I shall, as I have said, mean reality—in other words, each thing's essence, insofar as it exists, and operates in a particular manner, and without paying any regard to its duration. For no given thing can be said to be more perfect, because it has passed a longer time in existence. The duration of things cannot be determined by their essence, for the essence of things involves no fixed and definite period of existence; but everything, whether it be more perfect or less perfect, will always be able to persist in existence with the same force wherewith it began to exist; wherefore, in this respect, all things are equal. . . .

Prop. 7:

An emotion can only be controlled or destroyed by another emotion contrary thereto, and with more power for controlling emotion.

PROOF: Emotion, insofar as it is referred to the mind, is an idea, whereby the mind affirms of its body a greater or less force of existence than before (cf. General Definition of the Emotions at the end of Part III). When, therefore, the mind is assailed by any emotion, the body is at the same time affected with a modification whereby its power of activity is increased or diminished. Now this modification of the body (IV: 5) receives from its cause the force for persistence in its being; which force can only be checked or destroyed by a bodily cause (II: 6), in virtue of the body being affected with a modification contrary to (III: 5) and stronger than itself (IV: ax); wherefore (II, 12) the mind is affected by the idea of a modification contrary to, and stronger than the former modification, in other words, (by the General Definition of the Emotions) the mind will be affected by an emotion contrary to and stronger than the former emotion, which will exclude or destroy the existence of the former emotion; thus an emotion cannot be destroyed nor controlled except by a contrary and stronger emotion. QED.

COROLLARY: An emotion, insofar as it is referred to the mind, can only be controlled or destroyed through an idea of a modification of the body contrary to, and stronger than, that which we are undergoing. For the emotion which we undergo can only be checked or destroyed by an emotion contrary to, and stronger than, itself, in other words, (by the General Definition of the Emotions) only by an idea of a modification of the body contrary to, and stronger than, the modification which we undergo.

PROP. 8:

The knowledge of good and evil is nothing else but the emotions of pleasure or pain, insofar as we are conscious thereof.

PROOF: We call a thing good or evil, when it is of service or the reverse in preserving our being (IV: def1, def2), that is (III: 7), when it increases or diminishes, helps or hinders, our power of activity. Thus, insofar as we perceive that a thing affects us with pleasure or pain, we call it good or evil; wherefore the knowledge of good and evil is nothing else but the idea of the pleasure or pain, which necessarily follows from that pleasurable or painful emotion (II: 22). But this idea is united to the emotion in the same way as mind is united to body (II: 21); that is, there is no real distinction between this idea and the emotion or idea of the modification of the body, save in conception only. Therefore the knowledge of good and evil is nothing else but the emotion, insofar as we are conscious thereof. QED. . . .

PROP 14:

A true knowledge of good and evil cannot check any emotion by virtue of being true, but only insofar as it is considered as an emotion.

PROOF: An emotion is an idea, whereby the mind affirms of its body a greater or lesser force of existing than before (by III: General Definition of the Emotions); therefore it has no positive quality, which can be destroyed by the presence of what is true; consequently the knowledge of good and evil cannot, by virtue of being true, restrain any emotion. But, insofar as such knowledge is an emotion (IV: 8) if it have more strength for restraining emotion, it will to that extent be able to restrain the given emotion. QED.

PROP. 15:

Desire arising from the knowledge of good and bad can be quenched or checked by many of the other desires arising from the emotions whereby we are assailed.

PROOF: From the truc knowledge of good and evil, insofar as it is an emotion, necessarily arises desire (III: emot1), the strength of which is proportioned to the strength of the emotion wherefrom it arises (III: 37). But, inasmuch as this desire arises (by hypothesis) from the fact of our truly understanding anything, it follows that it is also present with us, insofar as we are active (III: 1), and must therefore be understood through our essence only (III: def2); consequently (III: 7) its force and increase can be defined solely by human power. Again, the desires arising from the emotions whereby we are assailed are stronger, in proportion as the said emotions are more vehement; wherefore their force and increase must be defined solely by the power of external causes, which, when compared with our own power, indefinitely surpass it (IV: 3); hence the desires arising from like emotions may be more vehement, than the desire which arises from a true knowledge of good and evil, and may, consequently, control or quench it. QED.

Prop. 16:

Desire arising from the knowledge of good and evil, insofar as such knowledge regards what is future, may be more easily controlled or quenched, than the desire for what is agreeable at the present moment.

proof: Emotion towards a thing, which we conceive as future, is fainter than emotion towards a thing that is present (IV: 9 c). But desire, which arises from the true knowledge of good and evil, though it be concerned with things which are good at the moment, can be quenched or controlled by any headstrong desire (by the last Prop., the proof whereof is of universal application). Wherefore desire arising from such knowledge, when concerned with the future, can be more easily controlled or quenched, etc. QED.

Prop. 17:

Desire arising from the true knowledge of good and evil, insofar as such knowledge is concerned with what is contingent, can be controlled far more easily still, than desire for things that are present.

PROOF: This Prop. is proved in the same way as the last Prop. from IV: 12 c.

NOTE: I think I have now shown the reason, why men are moved by opinion more readily than by true reason, why it is that the true knowledge of good and evil stirs up conflicts in the soul, and often yields to every kind of passion. This state of things gave rise to the exclamation of the poet:

> The better path I gaze at and approve,
> The worse—I follow.

Ecclesiastes seems to have had the same thought in his mind, when he says, "He who increaseth knowledge increaseth sorrow." I have not written the above with the object of drawing the conclusion, that ignorance is more excellent than knowledge, or that a wise man is on a par with a fool in controlling his emotions, but because it is necessary to know the power and the infirmity of our nature, before we can determine what reason can do in restraining the emotions, and what is beyond her power. I have said that in the present part I shall merely treat of human infirmity. The power of reason over the emotions I have settled to treat separately.

PROP. 18:

Desire arising from pleasure is, other conditions being equal, stronger than desire arising from pain.

PROOF: Desire is the essence of a man (III: emot1), that is, the endeavor whereby a man endeavors to persist in his own being. Wherefore desire arising from pleasure is, by the fact of pleasure being felt, increased or helped; on the contrary, desire arising from pain is, by the fact of pain being felt, diminished or hindered; hence the force of desire arising from pleasure must be defined by human power together with the power of an external cause, whereas desire arising from pain must be defined by human power only. Thus the former is the stronger of the two. QED.

NOTE: In these few remarks I have explained the causes of human infirmity and inconstancy, and shown why men do not abide by the precepts of reason. It now remains for me to show what course is marked out for us by reason, which of the emotions are in harmony with the rules of human reason, and which of them are contrary thereto. But, before I begin to prove my propositions in detailed geometrical fashion, it is advisable to sketch them briefly in advance, so that everyone may more readily grasp my meaning.

As reason makes no demands contrary to nature, it demands, that every man should love himself, should seek that which is useful to him—I mean, that which is really useful to him, should desire everything which really brings man to greater perfection, and should, each for himself, endeavor as far as he can to preserve his own being. This is as necessarily true, as that a whole is greater than its part (cf. III: 4).

Again, as virtue is nothing else but action in accordance with the laws of one's own nature (IV: def8), and as no one endeavors to preserve his own being, except in accordance with the laws of his own nature, it follows, *first*, that the foundation of virtue is the endeavor to preserve one's own being, and that happiness consists in man's power of preserving his own being; *secondly*, that virtue is to be desired for its own sake, and that there is nothing more excellent or more useful to us, for the sake of which we should desire it; *thirdly* and lastly, that suicides are weak-minded, and are overcome by external causes repugnant to their nature. Further, it follows from II: post4 that we can never arrive at doing without all external things for the preservation of our being or living, so as to have no relations with things which are outside ourselves. Again, if we consider our mind, we see that our intellect would be more imperfect, if mind were alone, and could understand nothing besides itself. There are, then, many things outside ourselves, which are useful to us, and are, therefore, to be desired. Of such none can be discerned more excellent, than those which are in entire agreement with our nature. For if, for example, two individuals of entirely the same nature are united, they form a combination twice as powerful as either of them singly.

Therefore, to man there is nothing more useful than man—nothing, I repeat, more excellent for preserving their being can be wished for by men, than that all should so in all points agree, that the minds and bodies of all should form, as it were, one single mind and one single body, and that all should, with one consent, as far as they are able, endeavor to preserve their being, and all with one consent seek what is useful to them all. Hence, men who are governed by reason—that is, who seek what is useful to them in accordance with reason—desire for themselves nothing, which they do not also desire for the rest of mankind, and, consequently, are just, faithful, and honorable in their conduct.

Such are the dictates of reason, which I purposed thus briefly to indicate, before beginning to prove them in greater detail. I have taken this course, in order, if possible, to gain the attention of those who believe that the principle that every man is bound to seek what is useful for himself is the foundation of impiety, rather than of piety and virtue.

Therefore, after briefly showing that the contrary is the case, I go on to prove it by the same method, as that whereby I have hitherto proceeded.

PROP. 19:

Every man, by the laws of his nature, necessarily desires or shrinks from that which he deems to be good or bad.

PROOF: The knowledge of good and evil is (IV: 8) the emotion of pleasure or pain, insofar as we are conscious thereof; therefore, every man necessarily desires what he thinks good, and shrinks from what he thinks bad. Now this appetite is nothing else but man's nature or essence (cf. the definition of Appetite in III: 9 n; and III: emot1). Therefore, every man, solely by the laws of his nature, desires the one, and shrinks from the other, etc. QED.

PROP. 20:

The more every man endeavors, and is able to seek what is useful to him—in other words, to preserve his own being—the more is he endowed with virtue; on the contrary, in proportion as a man neglects to seek what is useful to him, that is, to preserve his own being, he is wanting in power.

PROOF: Virtue is human power, which is defined solely by man's essence (IV: def8), that is, which is defined solely by the endeavor made by man to persist in his own being. Wherefore, the more a man endeavors, and is able to preserve his own being, the more is he endowed with virtue, and, consequently

(III: 4, 5), insofar as a man neglects to preserve his own being, he is wanting in power. QED.

NOTE: No one, therefore, neglects seeking his own good, or preserving his own being, unless he be overcome by causes external and foreign to his nature. No one, I say, from the necessity of his own nature, or otherwise than under compulsion from external causes, shrinks from food, or kills himself: which latter may be done in a variety of ways. A man, for instance, kills himself under the compulsion of another man, who twists round his right hand, wherewith he happened to have taken up a sword, and forces him to turn the blade against his own heart; or, again, he may be compelled, like Seneca, by a tyrant's command, to open his own veins—that is, to escape a greater evil by incurring a lesser; or, lastly, latent external causes may so disorder his imagination, and so affect his body, that it may assume a nature contrary to its former one, and whereof the idea cannot exist in the mind (III: 10). But that a man, from the necessity of his own nature, should endeavor to become nonexistent, is as impossible as that something should be made out of nothing, as everyone will see for himself, after a little reflection.

PROP. 21:

No one can desire to be blessed, to act rightly, and to live rightly, without at the same time wishing to be, to act, and to live—in other words, to actually exist.

PROOF: The proof of this proposition, or rather the proposition itself, is self-evident, and is also plain from the definition of desire. For the desire of living, acting, etc., blessedly or rightly, is (III: emot1) the essence of man—that is (III: 7), the endeavor made by everyone to preserve his own being. Therefore, no one can desire, etc. QED.

PROP. 22:

No virtue can be conceived as prior to this endeavor to preserve one's own being.

PROOF: The effort for self-preservation is the essence of a thing (III: 7); therefore, if any virtue could be conceived as prior thereto, the essence of a thing would have to be conceived as prior to itself, which is obviously absurd. Therefore no virtue, etc. QED.

COROLLARY: The effort for self-preservation is the first and only foundation of virtue. For prior to this principle nothing can be conceived, and without it no virtue can be conceived.

PROP. 23:

Man, insofar as he is determined to a particular action because he has inadequate ideas, cannot be absolutely said to act in obedience to virtue; he can only be so described, insofar as he is determined for the action because he understands.

PROOF: Insofar as a man is determined to an action through having inadequate ideas, he is passive (III: 1), that is (III: def1, def3), he does something, which cannot be perceived solely through his essence, that is, (by IV: def8) which does not follow from his virtue. But, insofar as he is determined for an action because he understands, he is active; that is, he does something, which is perceived through his essence alone, or which adequately follows from his virtue. QED.

PROP. 24:

To act absolutely in obedience to virtue is in us the same thing as to act, to live, or to preserve one's being (these three terms are identical in meaning) in accordance with the dictates of reason on the basis of seeking what is useful to one's self.

PROOF: To act absolutely in obedience to virtue is nothing else but to act according to the laws of one's own nature. But we only act, insofar as we understand (III: 3): therefore to act in obedience to virtue is in us nothing else but to act, to live, or to preserve one's being in obedience to reason and that on the basis of seeking what is useful for us (IV: 22 c). QED.

PROP. 25:

No one wishes to preserve his being for the sake of anything else.

PROOF: The endeavor, wherewith everything endeavors to persist in its being, is defined solely by the essence of the thing itself (III: 7); from this alone, and not from the essence of anything else, it necessarily follows (III: 6) that everyone endeavors to preserve his being. Moreover, this proposition is plain from IV: 22 c, for if a man should endeavor to preserve his being for the sake of anything else, the last-named thing would obviously be the basis of virtue, which, by the foregoing corollary, is absurd. Therefore no one, etc. QED.

PROP. 26:

Whatsoever we endeavor in obedience to reason is nothing further than to understand; neither does the mind, insofar as it makes use of reason, judge anything to be useful to it, save such things as are conducive to understanding.

PROOF: The effort for self-preservation is nothing else but the essence of the thing in question (III: 7), which, insofar as it exists such as it is, is conceived to have force for continuing in existence (III: 6) and doing such things as necessarily follow from its given nature (see the definition of Appetite, III: 9 n). But the essence of reason is not else but our mind, insofar as it clearly and distinctly understands (see the definition in II: 40 n2); therefore (II: 40) whatsoever we endeavor in obedience to reason is nothing else but to understand. Again, since this effort of the mind wherewith the mind endeavors, insofar as it reasons, to preserve its own being is nothing else but understanding; this effort at understanding is (IV: 22 c) the first and single basis of virtue, nor shall we endeavor to understand things for the sake of any ulterior object (IV: 25); on the other hand, the mind, insofar as it reasons, will not be able to conceive any good for itself, save such things as are conducive to understanding.

PROP. 27:

We know nothing to be certainly good or evil, save such things as really conduce to understanding, or such as are able to hinder us from understanding.

PROOF: The mind, insofar as it reasons, desires nothing beyond understanding, and judges nothing to be useful to itself, save such things as conduce to understanding (by the foregoing Prop.). But the mind (II: 41, 43 and n) cannot possess certainty concerning anything, except insofar as it has adequate ideas, or (what by II: 40 n, is the same thing) insofar as it reasons. Therefore we know nothing to be good or evil save such things as really conduce, etc. QED.

PROP. 28:

The mind's highest good is the knowledge of God, and the mind's highest virtue is to know God.

PROOF: The mind is not capable of understanding anything higher than God, that is (I: def6), than a Being absolutely infinite, and without which (I: 15) nothing can either be or be conceived; therefore (IV: 26, 27), the mind's highest utility or (IV: def1) good is the knowledge of God. Again, the mind is active, only insofar as it understands, and only to the same extent can it be said absolutely to act virtuously. The mind's absolute virtue is therefore to understand. Now, as we have already shown, the highest that the mind can understand is God; therefore the highest virtue of the mind is to understand or to know God. QED.

PROP. 29:

No individual thing, which is entirely different from our own nature, can help or check our power of activity, and absolutely nothing can do us good or harm, unless it has something in common with our nature.

PROOF: The power of every individual thing, and consequently the power of man, whereby he exists and operates, can only be determined by an individual thing (I: 28), whose nature (II: 6) must be understood through the same nature as that through which human nature is conceived. Therefore our power of activity, however it be conceived, can be determined and consequently helped or hindered by the power of any other individual thing, which has something in common with us, but not by the power of anything of which the nature is entirely different from our own; and since we call good or evil that which is the cause of pleasure or pain (IV: 8), that is (III: 40 n), which increases or diminishes, helps or hinders, our power of activity; therefore, that which is entirely different from our nature can neither be to us good nor bad. QED.

PROP. 30:

A thing cannot be bad for us through the quality which it has in common with our nature, but it is bad for us insofar as it is contrary to our nature.

PROOF: We call a thing bad when it is the cause of pain (IV: 8), that is (by the definition in III: 11 n), when it diminishes or checks our power of action. Therefore, if anything were bad for us through that quality which it has in common with our nature, it would be able itself to diminish or check that which it has in common with our nature, which (III: 4) is absurd. Wherefore nothing can be bad for us through that quality which it has in common with us, but, on the other hand, insofar as it is bad for us, that is (as we have just shown), insofar as it can diminish or check our power of action, it is contrary to our nature. QED.

PROP. 31:

Insofar as a thing is in harmony with our nature, it is necessarily good.

PROOF: Insofar as a thing is in harmony with our nature, it cannot be bad for it. It will therefore necessarily be either good or indifferent. If it be assumed that it be neither good nor bad, nothing will follow from its nature (IV: def1), which tends to the preservation of our nature, that is (by the hypothesis), which tends to the preservation of the thing itself; but this (III: 6) is absurd; therefore, insofar as a thing is in harmony with our nature, it is necessarily good. QED.

COROLLARY: Hence it follows, that, in proportion as a thing is in harmony with our nature, so is it more useful or better for us, and *vice versa*, in proportion as a thing is more useful for us, so is it more in harmony with our nature. For, insofar as it is not in harmony with our nature, it will necessarily be different therefrom or contrary thereto. If different, it can neither be good nor bad (IV: 29); if contrary, it will be contrary to that which is in harmony with our nature, that is, contrary to what is good—in short, bad. Nothing, therefore, can be good, except insofar as it is in harmony with our nature; and hence a thing is useful, in proportion as it is in harmony with our nature, and *vice versa*. QED.

PROP. 32:

Insofar as men are a prey to passion, they cannot, in that respect, be said to be naturally in harmony.

PROOF: Things, which are said to be in harmony naturally, are understood to agree in power (III: 7), not in want of power or negation, and consequently not in passion (III: 3 n); wherefore men, insofar as they are a prey to their passions, cannot be said to be naturally in harmony. QED.

NOTE: This is also self-evident; for, if we say that white and black only agree in the fact that neither is red, we absolutely affirm that they do not agree in any respect. So, if we say that a man and a stone only agree in the fact that both are finite—wanting in power, not existing by the necessity of their own nature, or, lastly, indefinitely surpassed by the power of external causes—we should certainly affirm that a man and a stone are in no respect alike; therefore, things which agree only in negation, or in qualities which neither possess, really agree in no respect.

Prop. 33:

Men can differ in nature, insofar as they are assailed by those emotions, which are passions, or passive states; and to this extent one and the same man is variable and inconstant.

PROOF: The nature or essence of the emotions cannot be explained solely through our essence or nature (III: def1, def2), but it must be defined by the power, that is (III: 7), by the nature of external causes in comparison with our own; hence it follows, that there are as many kinds of each emotion as there are external objects whereby we are affected (III: 56), and that men may be differently affected by one and the same object (III: 51), and to this extent differ in nature; lastly, that one and the same man may be differently affected towards the same object, and may therefore be variable and inconstant. QED.

PROP. 34:

Insofar as men are assailed by emotions which are passions, they can be contrary one to another.

PROOF: A man, for instance Peter, can be the cause of Paul's feeling pain, because he (Peter) possesses something similar to that which Paul hates (III: 16), or because Peter has sole possession of a thing which Paul also loves (III: 32 and n), or for other causes (of which the chief are enumerated in III: 55 n); it may therefore happen that Paul should hate Peter (III: emot7), consequently it may easily happen also, that Peter should hate Paul in return, and that each should endeavor to do the other an injury (III: 39), that is (IV: 30), that they should be contrary one to another. But the emotion of pain is always a passion or passive state (III: 59); hence men, insofar as they are assailed by emotions which are passions, can be contrary one to another. QED.

NOTE: I said that Paul may hate Peter, because he conceives that Peter possesses something which he (Paul) also loves; from this it seems, at first sight, to follow, that these two men, through both loving the same thing, and, consequently, through agreement of their respective natures, stand in one another's way; if this were so, Props. 30 and 31 of this Part would be untrue. But if we give the matter our unbiased attention, we shall see that the discrepancy vanishes. For the two men are not in one another's way in virtue of the agreement of their natures, that is, through both loving the same thing, but in virtue of one differing from the other. For, insofar as each loves the same thing, the love of each is fostered thereby (III: 31), that is (III: emot6) the pleasure of each is fostered thereby. Wherefore it is far from being the case, that they are at variance through both loving the same thing, and through the agreement in their natures. The cause for their opposition lies, as I have said, solely in the fact that they are assumed to differ. For we assume that Peter has the idea of the loved object as already in his possession, while Paul has the idea of the loved object as lost. Hence the one man will be affected with pleasure, the other will be affected with pain, and thus they will be at variance one with another. We can easily show in like manner, that all other causes of hatred depend solely on differences, and not on the agreement between men's natures.

PROP. 35:

Insofar only as men live in obedience to reason, do they always necessarily agree in nature.

PROOF: Insofar as men are assailed by emotions that are passions, they can be different in nature (IV: 33), and at variance one with another. But men are only said to be active, insofar as they act in obedience to reason (III: 3); therefore, whatsoever follows from human nature insofar as it is defined by reason must (III: def2) be understood solely through human nature as its proximate cause. But, since every man by the laws of his nature desires that which he deems good, and endeavors to remove that which he deems bad (IV: 19); and further, since that which we, in accordance with reason, deem good or bad, necessarily is good or bad (II: 41); it follows that men, insofar as they live in obedience to reason, necessarily do only such things as are necessarily good for human nature, and consequently for each individual man (IV: 31 c); in other words, such things as are in harmony with each man's nature. Therefore, men insofar as they live in obedience to reason, necessarily live always in harmony one with another. QED.

COROLLARY 1: There is no individual thing in nature, which is more useful to man, than a man who lives in obedience to reason. For that thing is to man most useful, which is most in harmony with his nature (IV: 31 c); that is, obviously, man. But man acts absolutely according to the laws of his nature, when he lives in obedience to reason (III: def2), and to this extent only is always necessarily in harmony with the nature of another man (by the last Prop.); wherefore among individual things nothing is more useful to man, than a man who lives in obedience to reason. QED.

COROLLARY 2: As every man seeks most that which is useful to him, so are men most useful one to another. For the more a man seeks what is useful to him and endeavors to preserve himself, the more is he endowed with virtue (IV: 20), or, what is the same thing (IV: def8), the more is he endowed with power to act according to the laws of his own nature, that is to live in obedience to reason. But men are most in natural harmony when they live in obedience to reason (by the last Prop.); therefore (by the foregoing corollary) men will be most useful one to another, when each seeks most that which is useful to him. QED.

NOTE: What we have just shown is attested by experience so conspicuously that it is in the mouth of nearly everyone: "Man is to man a God." Yet it rarely happens that men live in obedience to reason, for things are so ordered among them, that they are generally envious and troublesome one to another. Nevertheless they are scarcely able to lead a solitary life, so that the definition of man as a social animal has met with general assent; in fact, men do derive from social life much more convenience than injury. Let satirists then laugh their fill at human affairs, let theologians rail, and let misanthropes praise to their utmost the life of untutored rusticity, let them heap contempt on men and praises on beasts; when all is said, they will find that men can provide for their wants much more easily by mutual help, and that only by uniting their forces can they escape from the dangers that on every side beset them: not to say how much more excellent and worthy of our knowledge it is, to study the actions of men than the actions of beasts. But I will treat of this more at length elsewhere.

PROP. 36:

The highest good of those who follow virtue is common to all, and therefore all can equally rejoice therein.

PROOF: To act virtuously is to act in obedience with reason (IV: 24), and whatsoever we endeavor to do in obedience to reason is to understand (IV: 26); therefore (IV: 28) the highest good for those who follow after virtue is to know God; that is (II: 47 and n) a good which is common to all and can be possessed by all men equally, insofar as they are of the same nature. QED.

NOTE: Someone may ask how it would be, if the highest good of those who follow after virtue were not common to all? Would it not then follow, as above (IV: 34), that men living in obedience to reason, that is (IV: 35), men insofar as they agree in nature, would be at variance one with another? To such an inquiry I make answer, that it follows not accidentally but from the very nature of reason, that man's highest good is common to all, inasmuch as it is deduced from the very essence of man, insofar as defined by reason; and that a man could neither be, nor be conceived without the power of taking pleasure in this highest good. For it belongs to the essence of the human mind (II: 47) to have an adequate knowledge of the eternal and infinite essence of God.

PROP. 37:

The good which every man, who follows after virtue, desires for himself he will also desire for other men, and so much the more, in proportion as he has a greater knowledge of God.

PROOF: Men, insofar as they live in obedience to reason, are most useful to their fellow men (IV: 35 c1); therefore (IV: 19), we shall in obedience to reason necessarily endeavor to bring about that men should live in obedience to reason. But the good which every man, insofar as he is guided by reason, or, in other words, follows after virtue, desires for himself, is to understand (IV: 26); wherefore the good, which each follower of virtue seeks for himself, he will desire also for others. Again, desire, insofar as it is referred to the mind, is the very essence of the mind (III: emot1); now the essence of the mind consists in knowledge (II: 11), which involves the knowledge of God (II: 47), and without it (I: 15), can neither be, nor be conceived; therefore, in proportion as the mind's essence involves a greater knowledge of God, so also will be greater the desire of the follower of virtue, that other men should possess that which he seeks as good for himself. QED.

ANOTHER PROOF: The good, which a man desires for himself and loves, he will love more constantly, if he sees that others love it also (III: 31); he will therefore endeavor that others should love it also; and as the good in question is common to all, and therefore all can rejoice therein, he will endeavor, for the same reason, to bring about that all should rejoice therein, and this he will do the more (III: 37), in proportion as his own enjoyment of the good is greater.

NOTE 1: He who, guided by emotion only, endeavors to cause others to love what he loves himself, and to make the rest of the world live according to his own fancy, acts solely by impulse, and is, therefore, hateful, especially to those who take delight in something different, and accordingly study and, by similar impulse, endeavor, to make men live in accordance with what pleases themselves. Again, as the highest good sought by men under the guidance of emotion is often such, that it can only be possessed by a single individual, it follows that those who love it are not consistent in their intentions, but, while they delight to sing its praises, fear to be believed. But he, who endeavors to lead men by reason, does not act by impulse but courteously and kindly, and his intention is always consistent. Again, whatsoever we desire and do, whereof we are the cause insofar as we possess the idea of God, or know God, I set down to *Religion*. The desire of well-doing, which is engendered by a life according to reason, I call *piety*. Further, the desire, whereby a man living according to reason is bound to associate others with himself in friendship, I call *honor*; by *honorable* I mean that which is praised by men living according to reason, and by *base* I mean that which is repugnant to the gaining of friendship. I have also shown in addition what are the foundations of a state; and the difference between true virtue and infirmity may be readily gathered from what I have said; namely, that true virtue is nothing else but living in accordance with reason; while infirmity is nothing else but man's allowing himself to be led by things which are external to himself, and to be by them determined to act in a manner demanded by the general disposition of things rather than by his own nature considered solely in itself.

Such are the matters which I engaged to prove in IV:
18, whereby it is plain that the law against the slaugh-
tering of animals is founded rather on vain superstition
and womanish pity than on sound reason. The rational
quest of what is useful to us further teaches us the necessity of associating ourselves with our fellowmen, but not
with beasts, or things, whose nature is different from our
own; we have the same rights in respect to them as they
have in respect to us. Nay, as everyone's right is defined
by his virtue, or power, men have far greater rights over
beasts than beasts have over men. Still I do not deny
that beasts feel: what I deny is, that we may not consult
our own advantage and use them as we please, treating
them in the way which best suits us; for their nature is
not like ours, and their emotions are naturally different
from human emotions (III: 57 n). It remains for me to
explain what I mean by just and unjust, sin and merit.
On these points see the following note.

NOTE 2: In the Appendix to Part I, I undertook to
explain praise and blame, merit and sin, justice and
injustice.

Concerning praise and blame I have spoken in III:
29 n: the time has now come to treat of the remaining terms. But I must first say a few words concerning
man in the state of nature and in society.

Every man exists by sovereign natural right, and, consequently, by sovereign natural right performs those
actions which follow from the necessity of his own

nature; therefore by sovereign natural right every man judges what is good and what is bad, takes care of his own advantage according to his own disposition (IV: 19, 20), avenges the wrongs done to him (III: 40 c2), and endeavors to preserve that which he loves and to destroy that which he hates (III: 28). Now, if men lived under the guidance of reason, everyone would remain in possession of this his right, without any injury being done to his neighbor (IV: 35 c1). But seeing that they are a prey to their emotions, which far surpass human power or virtue (IV: 6), they are often drawn in different directions, and being at variance one with another (IV: 33, 34), stand in need of mutual help (IV, 35 n). Wherefore, in order that men may live together in harmony, and may aid one another, it is necessary that they should forego their natural right, and, for the sake of security, refrain from all actions which can injure their fellowmen. The way in which this end can be attained, so that men who are necessarily a prey to their emotions (IV, 4 c), inconstant and diverse, should be able to render each other mutually secure, and feel mutual trust, is evident from IV: 7; III: 39. It is there shown, that an emotion can only be restrained by an emotion stronger than, and contrary to itself, and that men avoid inflicting injury through fear of incurring a greater injury themselves.

On this law society can be established, so long as it keeps in its own hand the right, possessed by everyone, of avenging injury, and pronouncing on good and evil; and provided it also possesses the power to lay down a general rule of conduct, and to pass laws sanctioned, not by reason, which is powerless in restraining emotion, but by threats (IV: 17 n). Such a society established with laws and the power of preserving itself is called a *State*, while those who live under its protection are called *citizens*. We may readily understand that there is in the state of nature nothing, which by universal consent is pronounced good or bad; for in the state of nature everyone thinks solely of his own advantage, and according to his disposition, with reference only to his individual advantage, decides what is good or bad, being bound by no law to anyone besides himself.

In the state of nature, therefore, sin is inconceivable; it can only exist in a state, where good and evil are pronounced on by common consent, and where everyone is bound to obey the State authority. *Sin*, then, is nothing else but disobedience, which is therefore punished by the right of the State only. Obedience, on the other hand, is set down as *merit*, inasmuch as a man is thought worthy of merit, if he takes delight in the advantages which a State provides.

Again, in the state of nature, no one is by common consent master of anything, nor is there anything in nature, which can be said to belong to one man rather than another: all things are common to all. Hence, in the state of nature, we can conceive no wish to render to every man his own, or to deprive a man of that which belongs to him; in other words, there is nothing in the state of nature answering to justice and injustice. Such ideas are only possible in a social state, when it is decreed by common consent what belongs to one man and what to another.

From all these considerations it is evident, that justice and injustice, sin and merit, are extrinsic ideas, and not attributes which display the nature of the mind. But I have said enough....

PROP. 40:

Whatsoever conduces to man's social life, or causes men to live together in harmony, is useful, whereas whatsoever brings discord into a State is bad.

PROOF: For whatsoever causes men to live together in harmony also causes them to live according to reason (IV: 35), and is therefore (IV: 26; 27) good, and (for the same reason) whatsoever brings about discord is bad. QED.

PROP. 41:

Pleasure in itself is not bad but good: contrariwise, pain in itself is bad.

PROOF: Pleasure (III: 11 and n) is emotion, whereby the body's power of activity is increased or helped; pain is emotion, whereby the body's power of activity is diminished or checked; therefore (IV: 38) pleasure in itself is good, etc. QED.

PROP. 42:

Mirth cannot be excessive, but is always good; contrariwise, Melancholy is always bad.

PROOF: Mirth (see its definition in III: 11 n) is pleasure, which, insofar as it is referred to the body, consists in all parts of the body being affected equally: that is (III: 11), the body's power of activity is increased or aided in such a manner, that the several parts maintain their former proportion of motion and rest; therefore Mirth is always good (IV: 39), and cannot be excessive. But Melancholy (see its definition in III: 11 n) is pain, which, insofar as it is referred to the body, consists in the absolute decrease or hindrance of the body's power of activity; therefore (IV: 38) it is always bad. QED.

PROP. 43:

Stimulation may be excessive and bad; on the other hand, grief may be good, insofar as stimulation or pleasure is bad.

PROOF: Localized pleasure or stimulation (*titillatio*) is pleasure, which, insofar as it is referred to the body, consists in one or some of its parts being affected more than the rest (see its definition,

III: 11 n); the power of this emotion may be sufficient to overcome other actions of the body (IV: 6), and may remain obstinately fixed therein, thus rendering it incapable of being affected in a variety of other ways: therefore (IV: 38) it may be bad. Again, grief, which is pain, cannot as such be good (IV: 41). But, as its force and increase is defined by the power of an external cause compared with our own (IV: 5), we can conceive infinite degrees and modes of strength in this emotion (IV: 3); we can, therefore, conceive it as capable of restraining stimulation, and preventing its becoming excessive, and hindering the body's capabilities; thus, to this extent, it will be good. QED.

PROP. 44:

Love and desire may be excessive.

PROOF: Love is pleasure, accompanied by the idea of an external cause (III: emot6); therefore stimulation, accompanied by the idea of an external cause is love (III: 11 n); hence love may be excessive. Again, the strength of desire varies in proportion to the emotion from which it arises (III: 37). Now emotion may overcome all the rest of men's actions (IV: 6); so, therefore, can desire, which arises from the same emotion, overcome all other desires, and become excessive, as we showed in the last proposition concerning stimulation.

NOTE: Mirth, which I have stated to be good, can be conceived more easily than it can be observed. For the emotions, whereby we are daily assailed, are generally referred to some part of the body which is affected more than the rest; hence the emotions are generally excessive, and so fix the mind in the contemplation of one object, that it is unable to think of others; and although men, as a rule, are a prey to many emotions—and very few are found who are always assailed by one and the same—yet there are cases, where one and the same emotion remains obstinately fixed. We sometimes see men so absorbed in one object, that, although it be not present, they think they have it before them; when this is the case with a man who is not asleep, we say he is delirious or mad; nor are those persons who are inflamed with love, and who dream all night and all day about nothing but their mistress, or some woman, considered as less mad, for they are made objects of ridicule. But when a miser thinks of nothing but gain or money, or when an ambitious man thinks of nothing but glory, they are not reckoned to be mad, because they are generally harmful, and are thought worthy of being hated. But, in reality, Avarice, Ambition, Lust, etc., are species of madness, though they may not be reckoned among diseases.

PROP. 45:

Hatred can never be good.

PROOF: When we hate a man, we endeavor to destroy him (III: 39), that is (IV: 37), we endeavor to do something that is bad. Therefore, etc. QED.

NB. Here, and in what follows, I mean by hatred only hatred towards men.

COROLLARY 1: Envy, derision, contempt, anger, revenge, and other emotions attributable to hatred or arising therefrom, are bad; this is evident from III: 39 and IV: 37.

COROLLARY 2: Whatsoever we desire from motives of hatred is base, and in a State unjust. This also is evident from III: 39, and from the definitions of baseness and injustice in IV: 37 n.

NOTE: Between derision (which I have in Corollary 1 stated to be bad) and laughter I recognize a great difference. For laughter, as also jocularity, is merely pleasure; therefore, so long as it be not excessive, it is in itself good (IV: 41). Assuredly nothing forbids man to enjoy himself, save grim and gloomy superstition. For why is it more lawful to satiate one's hunger and thirst than to drive away one's melancholy? I reason, and have convinced myself as follows: No deity, nor anyone else, save the envious, takes pleasure in my infirmity and discomfort, nor sets down to my virtue the tears, sobs, fear, and the like, which are signs of infirmity of spirit; on the contrary, the greater the pleasure wherewith we are affected, the greater the perfection whereto we pass; in other words, the more must we necessarily partake of the divine nature. Therefore, to make use of what comes in our way, and to enjoy it as much as possible (not to the point of satiety, for that would not be enjoyment) is the part of a wise man. I say it is the part of a wise man to refresh and recreate himself with moderate and pleasant food and drink, and also with perfumes, with the soft beauty of growing plants, with dress, with music, with many sports, with theaters, and the like, such as every man may make use of without injury to his neighbor. For the human body is composed of very numerous parts, of diverse nature, which continually stand in need of fresh and varied nourishment, so that the whole body may be equally capable of performing all the actions, which follow from the necessity of its own nature; and, consequently, so that the mind may also be equally capable of understanding many things simultaneously. This way of life, then, agrees best with our principles, and also with general practice; therefore, if there be any question of another plan, the plan we have mentioned is the best, and in every way to be commended. There is no need for me to set forth the matter more clearly or in more detail. . . .

NOTE: He who chooses to avenge wrongs with hatred is assuredly wretched. But he, who strives to conquer hatred with love, fights his battle in joy and confidence; he withstands many as easily as one, and has very little need of fortune's aid. Those whom he vanquishes yield joyfully, not through failure, but through increase in their powers; all these consequences follow so plainly from the mere definitions of love and understanding, that I have no need to prove them in detail.

PROP. 47:

Emotions of hope and fear cannot be in themselves good.

PROOF: Emotions of hope and fear cannot exist without pain. For fear is pain (III: emot 13), and hope (III: emot 12, emot 13, explanation) cannot exist without fear; therefore (IV: 41) these emotions cannot be good in themselves, but only insofar as they can restrain excessive pleasure (IV: 43). QED.

NOTE: We may add that these emotions show defective knowledge and an absence of power in the mind; for the same reason confidence, despair, joy, and disappointment are signs of a want of mental power. For although confidence and joy are pleasurable emotions, they nevertheless imply a preceding pain, namely, hope and fear. Wherefore the more we endeavor to be guided by reason, the less do we depend on hope; we endeavor to free ourselves from fear, and, as far as we can, to dominate fortune, directing our actions by the sure counsels of wisdom.

Prop. 48:

The emotions of over-esteem and disparagement are always bad.

proof: These emotions (see III: emot21, emot22) are repugnant to reason; and are therefore (IV: 26, 27) bad. QED.

Prop. 49:

Over-esteem is apt to render its object proud.

proof: If we see that any one rates us too highly, for love's sake, we are apt to become elated (III: 41), or to be pleasurably affected (III: emot30); the good which we hear of ourselves we readily believe (III: 25); and therefore, for love's sake, rate ourselves too highly; in other words, we are apt to become proud. QED.

Prop. 50:

Pity, in a man who lives under the guidance of reason, is in itself bad and useless.

proof: Pity (III: emot18) is a pain, and therefore (IV: 41) is in itself bad. The good effect which follows, namely, our endeavor to free the object of our pity from misery, is an action which we desire to do solely at the dictation of reason (IV: 37); only at the dictation of reason are we able to perform any action, which we know for certain to be good (IV: 27); thus, in a man who lives under the guidance of reason, pity in itself is useless and bad. QED.

NOTE: He who rightly realizes that all things follow from the necessity of the divine nature, and come to pass in accordance with the eternal laws and rules of nature, will not find anything worthy of hatred, derision, or contempt, nor will he bestow pity on anything, but to the utmost extent of human virtue he will endeavor to do well, as the saying is, and to rejoice. We may add, that he, who is easily touched with compassion, and is moved by another's sorrow or tears, often does something which he afterwards regrets; partly because we can never be sure that an action caused by emotion is good, partly because we are easily deceived by false tears. I am in this place expressly speaking of a man living under the guidance of reason. He, who is moved to help others neither by reason nor by compassion, is rightly styled inhuman, for (III: 27) he seems unlike a man.

PROP. 51:

Approval is not repugnant to reason, but can agree therewith and arise therefrom.

PROOF: Approval is love towards one who has done good to another (III: emot19); therefore it may be referred to the mind, insofar as the latter is active (III: 59), that is (III: 3), insofar as it understands; therefore, it is in agreement with reason, etc. QED.

ANOTHER PROOF: He, who lives under the guidance of reason, desires for others the good which he seeks for himself (IV: 37); wherefore from seeing someone doing good to his fellow his own endeavor to do good is aided; in other words, he will feel pleasure (III: 11 n) accompanied by the idea of the benefactor. Therefore he approves of him. QED.

NOTE: Indignation as we defined it (III: emot20) is necessarily evil (IV: 45); we may, however, remark that when the sovereign power for the sake of preserving peace punishes a citizen who has injured another, it should not be said to be indignant with the criminal, for it is not incited by hatred to ruin him, it is led by a sense of duty to punish him.

Prop. 52:

Self-approval may arise from reason, and that which arises from reason is the highest possible.

PROOF: Self-approval is pleasure arising from a man's contemplation of himself and his own power of action (III: emot25). But a man's true power of action or virtue is reason herself (III: 3), as the said man clearly and distinctly contemplates her (II: 40; 43); therefore self-approval arises from reason. Again, when a man is contemplating himself, he only perceives clearly and distinctly or adequately, such things as follow from his power of action (III: def2), that is (III: 3), from his power of understanding; therefore in such contemplation alone does the highest possible self-approval arise. QED.

NOTE: Self-approval is in reality the highest object for which we can hope. For (as we showed in IV: 25) no one endeavors to preserve his being for the sake of any ulterior object, and, as this approval is more and more fostered and strengthened by praise (III: 53 c), and on the contrary (III: 55 c) is more and more disturbed by blame, fame becomes the most powerful of incitements to action, and life under disgrace is almost unendurable.

PROP. 53:

Humility is not a virtue, or does not arise from reason.

PROOF: Humility is pain arising from a man's contemplation of his own infirmities (III: emot26). But, insofar as a man knows himself by true reason, he is assumed to understand his essence, that is, his power (III: 7). Wherefore, if a man in self-contemplation perceives any infirmity in himself, it is not by virtue of his understanding himself, but (III: 55) by virtue of his power of activity being checked. But, if we assume that a man perceives his own infirmity by virtue of understanding something stronger than himself, by the knowledge of which he determines his own power of activity, this is the same as saying that we conceive that a man understands himself distinctly (IV: 26), because his power of activity is aided.

Wherefore humility, or the pain which arises from a man's contemplation of his own infirmity, does not arise from the contemplation or reason, and is not a virtue but a passion. QED.

PROP. 54:

Repentance is not a virtue, or does not arise from reason; but he who repents of an action is doubly wretched or infirm.

PROOF: The first part of this proposition is proved like the foregoing one. The second part is proved from the mere definition of the emotion in question (III: emot27). For the man allows himself to be overcome, first, by evil desires; secondly, by pain.

NOTE: As men seldom live under the guidance of reason, these two emotions, namely, Humility and Repentance, as also Hope and Fear, bring more good than harm; hence, as we must sin, we had better sin in that direction. For, if all men who are a prey to emotion were all equally proud, they would shrink from nothing, and would fear nothing; how then could they be joined and linked together in bonds of union? The crowd plays the tyrant, when it is not in fear; hence we need not wonder that the prophets, who consulted the good, not of a few, but of all, so strenuously commended Humility, Repentance, and Reverence. Indeed those who are a prey to these emotions may be led much more easily than others to live under the guidance of reason, that is, to become free and to enjoy the life of the blessed.

PROP. 55:

Extreme pride or dejection indicates extreme ignorance of self.

PROOF: This is evident from III: emot28, emot29.

PROP. 56:

Extreme pride or dejection indicates extreme infirmity of spirit.

PROOF: The first foundation of virtue is self-preservation (IV: 22 c) under the guidance of reason (IV: 24). He, therefore, who is ignorant of himself, is ignorant of the foundation of all virtues, and consequently of all virtues. Again, to act virtuously is merely to act under the guidance of reason (IV: 24): now he that acts under the guidance of reason must necessarily know that he so acts (II: 43). Therefore he who is in extreme ignorance of himself, and consequently of all virtues, acts least in obedience to virtue; in other words (IV: def8), is most infirm of spirit. Thus extreme pride or dejection indicates extreme infirmity of spirit. QED.

COROLLARY: Hence it most clearly follows, that the proud and the dejected specially fall a prey to the emotions.

NOTE: Yet dejection can be more easily corrected than pride; for the latter being a pleasurable emotion, and the former a painful emotion, the pleasurable is stronger than the painful (IV: 18).

PROP. 57:

The proud man delights in the company of flatterers and parasites, but hates the company of the high-minded.

PROOF: Pride is pleasure arising from a man's overestimation of himself (III: emot28, emot6); this estimation the proud man will endeavor to foster by all the means in his power (III: 13 n); he will therefore delight in the company of flatterers and parasites (whose character is too well known to need definition here), and will avoid the company of high-minded men, who value him according to his deserts. QED.

NOTE: It would be too long a task to enumerate here all the evil results of pride, inasmuch as the proud are a prey to all the emotions, though to none of them less than to love and pity. I cannot, however, pass over in silence the fact, that a man may be called proud from his underestimation of other people; and, therefore, pride in this sense may be defined as pleasure arising from the false opinion, whereby a man may consider himself superior to his fellows. The dejection, which is the opposite quality to this sort of pride, may be defined as pain arising from the false opinion, whereby a man may think himself inferior to his fellows. Such being the case, we can easily see that a proud man is necessarily envious (III: 41 n), and only takes pleasure in the company, who fool his weak mind to the top of his bent, and make him insane instead of merely foolish.

Though dejection is the emotion contrary to pride, yet is the dejected man very near akin to the proud man. For, inasmuch as his pain arises from a comparison between his own infirmity and other men's power or virtue, it will be removed, or, in other words, he will feel pleasure, if his imagination be occupied in contemplating other men's faults; whence arises the proverb, "The unhappy are comforted by finding fellow-sufferers." Contrariwise, he will be the more pained in proportion as he thinks himself inferior to others; hence none are so prone to envy as the dejected, they are specially keen in observing men's actions, with a view to fault-finding rather than correction, in order to reserve their praises for dejection, and to glory therein, though all the time with a dejected air. These effects follow as necessarily from the said emotion, as it follows from the nature of a triangle, that the three angles are equal to two right angles.

I have already said that I call these and similar emotions bad, solely in respect to what are useful to man. The laws of nature have regard to nature's general order, whereof man is but a part. I mention this, in passing, lest any should think that I have wished to set forth the faults and irrational deeds of men rather than the nature and properties of things. For, as I said in the preface to the third Part, I regard human emotions and their properties as on the same footing with other natural phenomena. Assuredly human emotions indicate the power and ingenuity of nature, if not of human nature, quite as fully as other things which we admire, and which we delight to contemplate. But I pass on to note those qualities in the emotions, which bring advantage to man, or inflict injury upon him.

PROP. 58:

Honor (gloria) is not repugnant to reason, but may arise therefrom.

PROOF: This is evident from III: emot30, and also from the definition of an honorable man (IV: 37 n1).

NOTE: Empty honor, as it is styled, is self-approval, fostered only by the good opinion of the populace; when this good opinion ceases there ceases also the self-approval, in other words, the highest object of each man's love (IV: 52 n); consequently, he whose honor is rooted in popular approval must, day by day, anxiously strive, act, and scheme in order to retain his reputation. For the populace is variable and inconstant, so that, if a reputation be not kept up, it quickly withers away. Everyone wishes to catch popular applause for himself, and readily represses the fame of others. The object of the strife being estimated as the greatest of all goods, each combatant is seized with a fierce desire to put down his rivals in every possible way, till he who at last comes out victorious is more proud of having done harm to others than of having done good to himself. This sort of honor, then, is really empty, being nothing.

The points to note concerning shame may easily be inferred from what was said on the subject of mercy and repentance. I will only add that shame, like compassion, though not a virtue is yet good, insofar as it shows that the feeler of shame is really imbued with the desire to live honorably; in the same way as suffering is good, as showing that the injured part is not mortified. Therefore, though a man who feels shame is sorrowful, he is yet more perfect than he, who is shameless, and has no desire to live honorably.

Such are the points which I undertook to remark upon concerning the emotions of pleasure and pain; as for the desires, they are good or bad according as they spring from good or evil emotions. But all, insofar as they are engendered in us by emotions wherein the mind is passive, are blind (as is evident from what was said in IV: 44 n), and would be useless, if men could easily be induced to live by the guidance of reason only, as I will now briefly show.

PROP. 59:

To all the actions, whereto we are determined by emotion wherein the mind is passive, we can be determined without emotion by reason.

PROOF: To act rationally is nothing else (III: 3 and def2) but to perform those actions, which follow from the necessity of our nature considered in itself alone. But pain is bad, insofar as it diminishes or checks the power of action (IV: 41); wherefore we cannot by pain be determined to any action, which we should be unable to perform under the guidance of reason. Again, pleasure is bad only insofar as it hinders a man's capability for action (IV: 41, 43); therefore to this extent we could not be determined by it to any action, which we could not perform under the guidance of reason. Lastly, pleasure, insofar as it is good, is in harmony with reason (for it consists in the fact that a man's capability for action is increased or aided); nor is the mind passive therein, except insofar as a man's power of action is not increased to the extent of affording him an adequate conception of himself and his actions (III: 3 and n).

Wherefore, if a man who is pleasurably affected be brought to such a state of perfection, that he gains an adequate conception of himself and his own actions, he will be equally, nay more, capable of those actions, to which he is determined by emotion wherein the mind is passive. But all emotions are attributable to pleasure, to pain, or to desire (III: emot4, explanation); and desire (III: emot1) is nothing else but the attempt to act; therefore, to all actions, etc. QED.

ANOTHER PROOF: A given action is called bad, insofar as it arises from one being affected by hatred or any evil emotion. But no action, considered in itself alone, is either good or bad (as we pointed out in the preface to Part IV), one and the same action being sometimes good, sometimes bad; wherefore to the action which is sometimes bad, or arises from some evil emotion, we may be led by reason (IV: 19). QED.

NOTE: An example will put this point in a clearer light. The action of striking, insofar as it is considered physically, and insofar as we merely look to the fact that a man raises his arm, clenches his fist, and moves his whole arm violently downwards, is a virtue or excellence which is conceived as proper to the structure of the human body. If, then, a man, moved by anger or hatred, is led to clench his fist or to move his arm, this result takes place (as we showed in Part II), because one and the same action can be associated with various mental images of things; therefore we may be determined to the performance of one and the same action by confused ideas, or by clear and distinct ideas. Hence it is evident that every desire which springs from emotion, wherein the mind is passive, would become useless, if men could be guided by reason.

Let us now see why desire which arises from emotion, wherein the mind is passive, is called by us blind.

PROP. 60:

Desire arising from a pleasure or pain that is not attributable to the whole body, but only to one or certain parts thereof, is without utility in respect to a man as a whole.

PROOF: Let it be assumed, for instance, that A, a part of a body, is so strengthened by some external cause that it prevails over the remaining parts (IV: 6). This part will not endeavor to do away with its own powers, in order that the other parts of the body may perform its office; for this it would be necessary for it to have a force or power of doing away with its own powers, which (III: 6) is absurd. The said part and, consequently, the mind also, will endeavor to preserve its condition. Wherefore desire arising from a pleasure of the kind aforesaid has no utility in reference to a man as a whole. If it be assumed, on the other hand, that the part, A, be checked so that the remaining parts prevail, it may be proved in the same manner that desire arising from pain has no utility in respect to a man as a whole. QED.

NOTE: As pleasure is generally (IV: 44 n) attributed to one part of the body, we generally desire to preserve our being without taking into consideration our health as a whole: to which it may be added, that the desires which have most hold over us (IV: 9) take account of the present and not of the future.

Prop. 61:

Desire which springs from reason cannot be excessive.

proof: Desire (III: emot1) considered absolutely is the actual essence of man, insofar as it is conceived as in any way determined to a particular activity by some given modification of itself. Hence desire, which arises from reason that is (III: 3), which is engendered in us insofar as we act, is the actual essence or nature of man, insofar as it is conceived as determined to such activities as are adequately conceived through man's essence only (III: def2). Now, if such desire could be excessive, human nature considered in itself alone would be able to exceed itself, or would be able to do more than it can, a manifest contradiction. Therefore, such desire cannot be excessive. QED.

Prop. 62:

Insofar as the mind conceives a thing under the dictates of reason, it is affected equally, whether the idea be of a thing future, past, or present.

proof: Whatsoever the mind conceives under the guidance of reason, it conceives under the form of eternity or necessity (II: 44 c2), and is therefore affected with the same certitude (II: 43 and n). Wherefore, whether the thing be present, past, or future, the mind conceives it under the same necessity and is affected with the same certitude; and whether the idea be of something present, past, or future, it will in all cases be equally true (II: 41); that is, it will always possess the same properties of an adequate idea (II: def4); therefore, insofar as the mind conceives things under the dictates of reason, it is affected in the same manner, whether the idea be of a thing future, past, or present. QED.

NOTE: If we could possess an adequate knowledge of the duration of things, and could determine by reason their periods of existence, we should contemplate things future with the same emotion as things present; and the mind would desire as though it were present the good which it conceived as future; consequently it would necessarily neglect a lesser good in the present for the sake of a greater good in the future, and would in no wise desire that which is good in the present but a source of evil in the future, as we shall presently show. However, we can have but a very inadequate knowledge of the duration of things (II: 31); and the periods of their existence (II: 44 n) we can only determine by imagination, which is not so powerfully affected by the future as by the present. Hence such true knowledge of good and evil as we possess is merely abstract or general, and the judgment which we pass on the order of things and the connection of causes, with a view to determining what is good or bad for us in the present, is rather imaginary than real. Therefore it is nothing wonderful, if the desire arising from such knowledge of good and evil, insofar as it looks on into the future, be more readily checked than the desire of things which are agreeable at the present time (cf. IV: 16).

Prop. 63:

He who is led by fear, and does good in order to escape evil, is not led by reason.

PROOF: All the emotions which are attributable to the mind as active, or in other words to reason, are emotions of pleasure and desire (III: 59); therefore, he who is led by fear, and does good in order to escape evil, is not led by reason.

NOTE: Superstitious persons, who know better how to rail at vice than how to teach virtue, and who strive not to guide men by reason, but so to restrain them that they would rather escape evil than love virtue, have no other aim but to make others as wretched as themselves; wherefore it is nothing wonderful, if they be generally troublesome and odious to their fellowmen.

COROLLARY: Under desire which springs from reason, we seek good directly, and shun evil indirectly.

PROOF: Desire which springs from reason can only spring from a pleasurable emotion, wherein the mind is not passive (III: 59), in other words, from a pleasure which cannot be excessive (IV: 61), and not from pain; wherefore this desire springs from the knowledge of good, not of evil (IV: 8); hence under the guidance of reason we seek good directly and only by implication shun evil. QED.

NOTE: This Corollary may be illustrated by the example of a sick and a healthy man. The sick man through fear of death eats what he naturally shrinks from, but the healthy man takes pleasure in his food, and thus gets a better enjoyment out of life, than if he was in fear of death, and desired directly to avoid it. So a judge, who condemns a criminal to death, not from hatred or anger but from love of the public well-being, is guided solely by reason.

PROP. 64:

The knowledge of evil is an inadequate knowledge.

PROOF: The knowledge of evil (IV: 8) is pain, insofar as we are conscious thereof. Now pain is the transition to a lesser perfection (III: emot3) and therefore cannot be understood through man's nature (III: 6, 7); therefore it is a passive state (III: def2) which (III: 3) depends on inadequate ideas; consequently the knowledge thereof (II: 29), namely, the knowledge of evil, is inadequate. QED.

COROLLARY: Hence it follows that, if the human mind possessed only adequate ideas, it would form no conception of evil.

PROP. 65:

Under the guidance of reason we should pursue the greater of two goods and the lesser of two evils.

PROOF: A good which prevents our enjoyment of a greater good is in reality an evil; for we apply the terms good and bad to things, insofar as we compare them one with another (see preface to this Part); therefore, evil is in reality a lesser good; hence under the guidance of reason we seek or pursue only the greater good and the lesser evil. QED.

COROLLARY: We may, under the guidance of reason, pursue the lesser evil as though it were the greater good, and we may shun the lesser good, which would be the cause of the greater evil. For the evil, which is here called the lesser, is really good, and the lesser good is really evil, wherefore we may seek the former and shun the latter. QED.

PROP. 66:

We may, under the guidance of reason, seek a greater good in the future in preference to a lesser good in the present, and we may seek a lesser evil in the present in preference to a greater evil in the future.

PROOF: If the mind could have an adequate knowledge of things future, it would be affected towards what is future in the same way as towards what is present (IV: 62); wherefore, looking merely to reason, as in this proposition we are assumed to do, there is no difference, whether the greater good or evil be assumed as present, or assumed as future; hence (IV: 65) we may seek a greater good in the future in preference to a lesser good in the present, etc. QED.

COROLLARY: We may, under the guidance of reason, seek a lesser evil in the present, because it is the cause of a greater good in the future, and we may shun a lesser good in the present, because it is the cause of a greater evil in the future. This Corollary is related to the foregoing Proposition as IV: 65 c is related to the said IV: 65.

NOTE: If these statements be compared with what we have pointed out concerning the strength of the emotions in this Part up to Prop. 18, we shall readily see the difference between a man, who is led solely by emotion or opinion, and a man, who is led by reason. The former, whether he will or no, performs actions whereof he is utterly ignorant; the latter is his own master and only performs such actions, as he knows are of primary importance in life, and therefore chiefly desires; wherefore I call the former a slave, and the latter a free man, concerning whose disposition and manner of life it will be well to make a few observations.

PROP. 67:

A free man thinks of death least of all things; and his wisdom is a meditation not of death but of life.

PROOF: A free man is one who lives under the guidance of reason, who is not led by fear (IV: 63), but who directly desires that which is good (IV: 63 c), in other words (IV: 24), who strives to act, to live, and to preserve his being on the basis of seeking his own true advantage; wherefore such a one thinks of nothing less than of death, but his wisdom is a meditation of life. QED.

PROP. 68:

If men were born free, they would, so long as they remained free, form no conception of good and evil.

PROOF: I call free him who is led solely by reason; he, therefore, who is born free, and who remains free, has only adequate ideas; therefore (IV: 64 c) he has no conception of evil, or consequently (good and evil being correlative) of good. QED.

NOTE: It is evident, from IV: 4, that the hypothesis of this Proposition is false and inconceivable, except insofar as we look solely to the nature of man, or rather to God; not insofar as the latter is infinite, but only insofar as he is the cause of man's existence.

This, and other matters which we have already proved, seem to have been signified by Moses in the history of the first man. For in that narrative no other power of God is conceived, save that whereby he created man, that is the power wherewith he provided solely for man's advantage; it is stated that God forbade man, being free, to eat of the tree of the knowledge of good and evil, and that, as soon as man should have eaten of it, he would straightway fear death rather than desire to live. Further, it is written that when man had found a wife, who was in entire harmony with his nature, he knew that there could be nothing in nature which could be more useful to him; but that after he believed the beasts to be like himself, he straightway began to imitate their emotions (III: 27), and to lose his freedom; this freedom was afterwards recovered by the patriarchs, led by the spirit of Christ; that is, by the idea of God, whereon alone it depends, that man may be free, and desire for others the good which he desires for himself, as we have shown above (IV: 37).

PROP. 69:

The virtue of a free man is seen to be as great, when it declines dangers, as when it overcomes them.

PROOF: Emotion can only be checked or removed by an emotion contrary to itself, and possessing more power in restraining emotion (IV: 7). But blind daring and fear are emotions, which can be conceived as equally great (IV: 5, 3): hence, no less virtue or firmness is required in checking daring than in checking fear (III: 59 n); in other words (III: emot40, emot41), the free man shows as much virtue, when he declines dangers, as when he strives to overcome them. QED.

COROLLARY: The free man is as courageous in timely retreat as in combat; or, a free man shows equal courage or presence of mind, whether he elects to give battle or to retreat.

NOTE: What courage (*animositas*) is, and what I mean thereby, I explained in III: 59 n. By danger I mean everything, which can give rise to any evil, such as pain, hatred, discord, etc.

PROP. 70:

The free man, who lives among the ignorant, strives, as far as he can, to avoid receiving favors from them.

PROOF: Everyone judges what is good according to his disposition (III: 39 n); wherefore an ignorant man, who has conferred a benefit on another, puts his own estimate upon it, and, if it appears to be estimated less highly by the receiver, will feel pain (III: 42). But the free man only desires to join other men to him in friendship (IV: 37), not repaying their benefits with others reckoned as of like value, but guiding himself and others by the free decision of reason, and doing only such things as he knows to be of primary importance. Therefore the free man, lest he should become hateful to the ignorant, or follow their desires rather than reason, will endeavor, as far as he can, to avoid receiving their favors.

NOTE: I say, *as far as he can*. For though men be ignorant, yet are they men, and in cases of necessity could afford us human aid, the most excellent of all things: therefore it is often necessary to accept favors from them, and consequently to repay such favors in kind; we must, therefore, exercise caution in declining favors, lest we should have the appearance of despising those who bestow them, or of being, from avaricious motives, unwilling to requite them, and so give ground for offense by the very fact of striving to avoid it. Thus, in declining favors, we must look to the requirements of utility and courtesy.

Prop. 71:

Only free men are thoroughly grateful one to another.

PROOF: Only free men are thoroughly useful one to another, and associated among themselves by the closest necessity of friendship (IV: 35 and c1), only such men endeavor, with mutual zeal of love, to confer benefits on each other (IV: 37), and, therefore, only they are thoroughly grateful one to another. QED.

NOTE: The goodwill, which men who are led by blind desire have for one another, is generally a bargaining or enticement, rather than pure goodwill. Moreover, ingratitude is not an emotion. Yet it is base, inasmuch as it generally shows, that a man is affected by excessive hatred, anger, pride, avarice, etc. He who, by reason of his folly, knows not how to return benefits, is not ungrateful, much less he who is not gained over by the gifts of a courtesan to serve her lust, or by a thief to conceal his thefts, or by any similar persons. Contrariwise, such a one shows a constant mind, inasmuch as he cannot by any gifts be corrupted, to his own or the general hurt.

Prop. 72:

The free man never acts fraudulently, but always in good faith.

proof: If it be asked: What should a man's conduct be in a case where he could by breaking faith free himself from the danger of present death? Would not his plan of self-preservation completely persuade him to deceive? This may be answered by pointing out that, if reason persuaded him to act thus, it would persuade all men to act in a similar manner, in which case reason would persuade men not to agree in good faith to unite their forces, or to have laws in common, that is, not to have any general laws, which is absurd.

Prop. 73:

The man, who is guided by reason, is more free in a State, where he lives under a general system of law, than in solitude, where he is independent.

proof: The man, who is guided by reason, does not obey through fear (IV: 63): but, insofar as he endeavors to preserve his being according to the dictates of reason, that is (IV: 66 n), insofar as he endeavors to live in freedom, he desires to order his life according to the general good (IV: 37), and, consequently (as we showed in IV: 37 n2), to live according to the laws of his country. Therefore the free man, in order to enjoy greater freedom, desires to possess the general rights of citizenship. QED.

note: These and similar observations, which we have made on man's true freedom, may be referred to strength, that is, to courage and nobility of character (III: 59 n). I do not think it worthwhile to prove separately all the properties of strength; much less need I show, that he that is strong hates no man, is angry with no man, envies no man, is indignant with no man, despises no man, and least of all things is proud. These propositions, and all that relate to the true way of life and religion, are easily proved from IV: 37, 46; namely, that hatred should be overcome with love, and that every man should desire for others the good which he seeks for himself. We may also repeat what we drew attention to in the note to IV: 1, and in other places; namely, that the strong man has ever first in his thoughts, that all things follow from the necessity of the divine nature; so that whatsoever he deems to be hurtful and evil, and whatsoever, accordingly, seems to him impious, horrible, unjust, and base, assumes that appearance owing to his own disordered, fragmentary, and confused view of the universe. Wherefore he strives before all things to conceive things as they really are, and to remove the hindrances to true knowledge, such as are hatred, anger, envy, derision, pride, and similar emotions, which I have mentioned above. Thus he endeavors, as we said before, as far as in him lies, to do good, and to go on his way rejoicing. How far human virtue is capable of attaining to such a condition, and what its powers may be, I will prove in the following Part.

Appendix C
The Power of Reason
(Gaining Human Freedom)

Part V: On the Power of the Understanding, or of Human Freedom

Prop. 3:

An emotion, which is a passion, ceases to be a passion, as soon as we form a clear and distinct idea thereof.

PROOF: An emotion, which is a passion, is a confused idea (by III: General Definition of the Emotions). If, therefore, we form a clear and distinct idea of a given emotion, that idea will only be distinguished from the emotion, insofar as it is referred to the mind only, by reason (II: 21 and n); therefore (III: 3), the emotion will cease to be a passion. QED.

corollary: An emotion therefore becomes more under our control, and the mind is less passive in respect to it, in proportion as it is more known to us.

Prop. 4:

There is no modification of the body, whereof we cannot form some clear and distinct conception.

proof: Properties which are common to all things can only be conceived adequately (II: 38); therefore (II, 12, 13 lemma 2) there is no modification of the body, whereof we cannot form some clear and distinct conception. QED.

corollary: Hence it follows that there is no emotion, whereof we cannot form some clear and distinct conception. For an emotion is the idea of a modification of the body (by III: General Definition of the Emotions), and must therefore (by the preceding Prop.) involve some clear and distinct conception.

note: Seeing that there is nothing which is not followed by an effect (I: 36), and that we clearly and distinctly understand whatever follows from an idea, which in us is adequate (II: 40), it follows that everyone has the power of clearly and distinctly understanding himself and his emotions, if not absolutely, at any rate in part, and consequently of bringing it about, that he should become less subject to them. To attain this result, therefore, we must chiefly direct our efforts to acquiring, as far as possible, a clear and distinct knowledge of every emotion, in order that the mind may thus, through emotion, be determined to think of those things which it clearly and distinctly perceives, and wherein it fully acquiesces: and thus that the emotion itself may be separated from the thought of an external cause, and may be associated with true thoughts; whence it will come to pass, not only that love, hatred, etc. will be destroyed (V: 2), but also that the appetites or desires, which are wont to arise from such emotion, will become incapable of being excessive (IV: 61). For it must be especially remarked, that the appetite through which a man is said to be active, and that through which he is said to be passive, is one and the same. For instance, we have shown that human nature is so constituted that everyone desires his fellowmen to live after his own fashion (III: 31 n); in a man, who is not guided by reason, this appetite is a passion which is called ambition, and does not greatly differ from pride; whereas in a man, who lives by the dictates of reason, it is an activity or virtue which is called piety (IV: 37 n1 and second proof). In like manner all appetites or desires are only passions, insofar as they spring from inadequate ideas; the same results are accredited to virtue, when they are aroused or generated by adequate ideas. For all desires, whereby we are determined to any given action may arise as much from adequate as from inadequate ideas (IV: 59). Than this remedy for the emotions (to return to the point from which I started), which consists in a true knowledge thereof, nothing more excellent, being within our power, can be devised. For the mind has no other power save that of thinking and of forming adequate ideas, as we have shown above (III: 3). . . .

Prop. 6:

The mind has greater power over the emotions and is less subject thereto, insofar as it understands all things as necessary.

proof: The mind understands all things to be necessary (I: 29) and to be determined to existence and operation by an infinite chain of causes; therefore (by the foregoing Proposition), it thus far brings it about, that it is less subject to the emotions arising therefrom, and (III: 48) feels less emotion towards the things themselves. QED.

note: The more this knowledge, that things are necessary, is applied to particular things, which we conceive more distinctly and vividly, the greater is the power of the mind over the emotions, as experience also testifies. For we see that the pain arising from the loss of any good is mitigated as soon as the man who has lost it perceives, that it could not by any means have been preserved. So also we see that no one pities an infant, because it cannot speak, walk, or reason, or lastly, because it passes so many years, as it were, in unconsciousness. Whereas, if most people were born full-grown and only one here and there as an infant, everyone would pity the infants; because infancy would not then be looked on as a state natural and necessary, but as a fault or delinquency in Nature; and we may note several other instances of the same sort. . . .

NOTE: . . . The best we can do, therefore, so long as we do not possess a perfect knowledge of our emotions, is to frame a system of right conduct, or fixed practical precepts, to commit it to memory, and to apply it forthwith to the particular circumstances which now and again meet us in life, so that our imagination may become fully imbued therewith, and that it may be always ready to our hand. For instance, we have laid down among the rules of life (IV: 46 and n), that hatred should be overcome with love or high-mindedness, and not requited with hatred in return. Now, that this precept of reason may be always ready to our hand in time of need, we should often think over and reflect upon the wrongs generally committed by men, and in what manner and way they may be best warded off by high-mindedness: we shall thus associate the idea of wrong with the idea of this precept, which accordingly will always be ready for use when a wrong is done to us (II: 18) If we keep also in readiness the notion of our true advantage, and of the good which follows from mutual friendships, and common fellowships; further, if we remember that complete acquiescence is the result of the right way of life (IV: 52), and that men, no less than everything else, act by the necessity of their nature: in such case I say the wrong, or the hatred, which commonly arises therefrom, will engross a very small part of our imagination and will be easily overcome; or, if the anger which springs from a grievous wrong be not overcome easily, it will nevertheless be overcome, though not without a spiritual conflict, far sooner than if we had not thus reflected on the subject beforehand. As is indeed evident from V: 6, 7, 8. We should, in the same way, reflect on courage as a means of overcoming fear; the ordinary dangers of life should frequently be brought to mind and imagined, together with the means whereby through readiness of resource and strength of mind we can avoid and overcome them. But we must note that in arranging our thoughts and conceptions we should always bear in mind that which is good in every individual thing (IV: 63 c; III: 59), in order that we may always be determined to action by an emotion of pleasure. For instance, if a man sees that he is too keen in the pursuit of honor, let him think over its right use, the end for which it should be pursued, and the means whereby he may attain it. Let him not think of its misuse, and its emptiness, and the fickleness of mankind, and the like, whereof no man thinks except through a morbidness of disposition; with thoughts like these do the most ambitious most torment themselves, when they despair of gaining the distinctions they hanker after, and in thus giving vent to their anger would fain appear wise. Wherefore it is certain that those, who cry out the loudest against the misuse of honor and the vanity of the world, are those who most greedily covet it. This is not peculiar to the ambitious, but is common to all who are ill-used by fortune, and who are infirm in spirit. For a poor man also, who is miserly, will talk incessantly of the misuse of wealth and of the vices of the rich; whereby he merely torments himself, and shows the world that he is intolerant, not only of his own poverty, but also of other people's riches. So, again, those who have been ill received by a woman they love think of nothing but the inconstancy, treachery, and other stock faults of the fair sex; all of which they consign to oblivion, directly they are again taken into favor by their sweetheart. Thus he who would govern his emotions and appetite solely by the love of freedom strives, as far as he can, to gain a knowledge of the virtues and their causes, and to fill his spirit with the joy which arises from the true knowledge of them: he will in no wise desire to dwell on men's faults, or to carp at his fellows, or to revel in a false show of freedom. Whosoever will diligently observe and practice these precepts (which indeed are not difficult) will verily, in a short space of time, be able, for the most part, to direct his actions according to the commandments of reason. . . .

PROP. 15:

He who clearly and distinctly understands himself and his emotions loves God, and so much the more in proportion as he more understands himself and his emotions.

PROOF: He who clearly and distinctly understands himself and his emotions feels pleasure (III: 53), and this pleasure is (by the last Prop.) accompanied by the idea of God; therefore (III: emot6) such a one loves God, and (for the same reason) so much the more in proportion as he more understands himself and his emotions. QED.

PROP 16:

This love towards God must hold the chief place in the mind.

PROOF: For this love is associated with all the modifications of the body (V: 14) and is fostered by them all (V: 15); therefore (V: 11), it must hold the chief place in the mind. QED.

PROP. 17:

God is without passions, neither is he affected by any emotion of pleasure or pain.

PROOF: All ideas, insofar as they are referred to God, are true (II: 32), that is (II: def4) adequate; and therefore (by III: General Definition of the Emotions) God is without passions. Again, God cannot pass either to a greater or to a lesser perfection (I: 20 c2); therefore (by III: emot2, emot3) he is not affected by any emotion of pleasure or pain.

COROLLARY: Strictly speaking, God does not love or hate anyone. For God (by the foregoing Prop.) is not affected by any emotion of pleasure or pain, consequently (III: emot6, emot7) he does not love or hate anyone.

PROP. 18:

No one can hate God.

PROOF: The idea of God which is in us is adequate and perfect (II: 46, 47); wherefore, insofar as we contemplate God, we are active (III: 3); consequently (III: 59) there can be no pain accompanied by the idea of God, in other words (III: emot7), no one can hate God. QED.

COROLLARY: Love towards God cannot be turned into hate.

NOTE: It may be objected that, as we understand God as the cause of all things, we by that very fact regard God as the cause of pain. But I make answer, that, insofar as we understand the causes of pain, it to that extent

(V: 3) ceases to be a passion, that is, it ceases to be pain (III: 59); therefore, insofar as we understand God to be the cause of pain, we to that extent feel pleasure.

Prop. 19:

He, who loves God, cannot endeavor that God should love him in return.

PROOF: For, if a man should so endeavor, he would desire (V: 17 c) that God, whom he loves, should not be God, and consequently he would desire to feel pain (III: 19); which is absurd (III: 28). Therefore, he who loves God, etc. QED.

Prop. 20:

This love towards God cannot be stained by the emotion of envy or jealousy: contrariwise, it is the more fostered, in proportion as we conceive a greater number of men to be joined to God by the same bond of love.

PROOF: This love towards God is the highest good which we can seek for under the guidance of reason (IV: 28), it is common to all men (IV: 36), and we desire that all should rejoice therein (IV: 37); therefore (III: emot23), it cannot be stained by the emotion of envy, nor by the emotion of jealousy (V: 18; see definition of Jealousy in III: 35 n); but, contrariwise, it must needs be the more fostered, in proportion as we conceive a greater number of men to rejoice therein. QED.

NOTE: We can in the same way show that there is no emotion directly contrary to this love, whereby this love can be destroyed; therefore we may conclude that this love towards God is the most constant of all the emotions, and that, insofar as it is referred to the body, it cannot be destroyed, unless the body be destroyed also. As to its nature, insofar as it is referred to the mind only, we shall presently inquire.

I have now gone through all the remedies against the emotions, or all that the mind, considered in itself alone, can do against them. Whence it appears that the mind's power over the emotions consists:

1. In the actual knowledge of the emotions (V: 4 n).
2. In the fact that it separates the emotions from the thought of an external cause, which we conceive confusedly (V: 2, 4 n).
3. In the fact, that, in respect to time, the emotions referred to things, which we distinctly understand, surpass those referred to what we conceive in a confused and fragmentary manner (V: 7).
4. In the number of causes whereby those modifications are fostered, which have regard to the common properties of things or to God (V: 9; 11).

5. Lastly, in the order wherein the mind can arrange and associate, one with another, its own emotions (V: 10 n, 12, 13, 14).

But, in order that this power of the mind over the emotions may be better understood, it should be specially observed that the emotions are called by us strong, when we compare the emotion of one man with the emotion of another, and see that one man is more troubled than another by the same emotion; or when we are comparing the various emotions of the same man one with another, and find that he is more affected or stirred by one emotion than by another. For the strength of every emotion is defined by a comparison of our own power with the power of an external cause. Now the power of the mind is defined by knowledge only, and its infirmity or passion is defined by the privation of knowledge only: it therefore follows, that that mind is most passive, whose greatest part is made up of inadequate ideas, so that it may be characterized more readily by its passive states than by its activities; on the other hand, that mind is most active, whose greatest part is made up of adequate ideas, so that, although it may contain as many inadequate ideas as the former mind, it may yet be more easily characterized by ideas attributable to human virtue, than by ideas which tell of human infirmity. Again, it must be observed, that spiritual unhealthiness and misfortunes can generally be traced to excessive love for something which is subject to many variations, and which we can never become masters of. For no one is solicitous or anxious about anything, unless he loves it; neither do wrongs, suspicions, enmities, etc. arise, except in regard to things whereof no one can be really master.

We may thus readily conceive the power which clear and distinct knowledge, and especially that third kind of knowledge (II: 47 n), founded on the actual knowledge of God, possesses over the emotions: if it does not absolutely destroy them, insofar as they are passions (V: 3, 4 n); at any rate, it causes them to occupy a very small part of the mind (V: 14). Further, it begets a love towards a thing immutable and eternal (V: 15), whereof we may really enter into possession (II: 45); neither can it be defiled with those faults which are inherent in ordinary love; but it may grow from strength to strength, and may engross the greater part of the mind, and deeply penetrate it.

And now I have finished with all that concerns this present life: for, as I said in the beginning of this note, I have briefly described all the remedies against the emotions. And this everyone may readily have seen for himself, if he has attended to what is advanced in the present note, and also to the definitions of the mind and its emotions, and, lastly, to III: 1, 3. It is now, therefore, time to pass on to those matters, which appertain to the duration of the mind, without relation to the body.

PROP. 21:

The mind can only imagine anything, or remember what is past, while the body endures.

PROOF: The mind does not express the actual existence of its body, nor does it imagine the modifications of the body as actual, except while the body endures (II: 8 c); and, consequently (II: 26), it does not imagine any body as actually existing, except while its own body endures. Thus it cannot imagine anything (for definition of Imagination, see II: 17 n), or remember things past, except while the body endures (see definition of Memory, II: 18 n). QED.

PROP. 22:

Nevertheless in God there is necessarily an idea, which expresses the essence of this or that human body under the form of eternity.

PROOF: God is the cause, not only of the existence of this or that human body, but also of its essence (I: 25). This essence, therefore, must necessarily be conceived through the very essence of God (I: ax4), and be thus conceived by a certain eternal necessity (I: 16); and this conception must necessarily exist in God (II: 3). QED.

PROP. 23:

The human mind cannot be absolutely destroyed with the body, but there remains of it something which is eternal.

PROOF: There is necessarily in God a concept or idea, which expresses the essence of the human body (last Prop.), which, therefore, is necessarily something appertaining to the essence of the human mind (II: 13). But we have not assigned to the human mind any duration, definable by time, except insofar as it expresses the actual existence of the body, which is explained through duration, and may be defined by time—that is (II: 8 c), we do not assign to it duration, except while the body endures. Yet, as there is something, notwithstanding, which is conceived by a certain eternal necessity through the very essence of God (last Prop.); this something, which appertains to the essence of the mind, will necessarily be eternal. QED.

NOTE: This idea, which expresses the essence of the body under the form of eternity, is, as we have said, a certain mode of thinking, which belongs to the essence of the mind, and is necessarily eternal. Yet it is not possible that we should remember that we existed before our body, for our body can bear no trace of such existence, neither can eternity be defined in terms of time, or have any relation to time. But, notwithstanding, we feel and know that we are eternal. For the mind feels those things that it conceives by understanding, no less than those things that it remembers. For the eyes of the mind, whereby it sees and observes things, are none other than proofs. Thus, although we do not remember that we existed before the body, yet we feel that our mind, insofar as it involves the essence of the body, under the form of eternity, is eternal, and that thus its existence cannot be defined in terms of time, or explained through duration. Thus our mind can only be said to endure, and its existence can only be defined by a fixed time, insofar as it involves the actual existence of the body. Thus far only has it the power of determining the existence of things by time, and conceiving them under the category of duration.

Prop. 24:

The more we understand particular things, the more do we understand God.

proof: This is evident from I: 25 c. . . .

note: Things are conceived by us as actual in two ways, either as existing in relation to a given time and place, or as contained in God and following from the necessity of the divine nature. Whatsoever we conceive in this second way as true or real, we conceive under the form of eternity, and their ideas involve the eternal and infinite essence of God, as we showed in II: 45 and n.

Prop. 30:

Our mind, insofar as it knows itself and the body under the form of eternity, has to that extent necessarily a knowledge of God, and knows that it is in God, and is conceived through God.

PROOF: Eternity is the very essence of God, insofar as this involves necessary existence (I: def8). Therefore to conceive things under the form of eternity, is to conceive things insofar as they are conceived through the essence of God as real entities, or insofar as they involve existence through the essence of God; wherefore our mind, insofar as it conceives itself and the body under the form of eternity, has to that extent necessarily a knowledge of God, and knows, etc. QED.

PROP. 31:

The third kind of knowledge depends on the mind, as its formal cause, insofar as the mind itself is eternal.

PROOF: The mind does not conceive anything under the form of eternity, except insofar as it conceives its own body under the form of eternity (V: 29); that is, except insofar as it is eternal (V: 21, 23); therefore (by the last Prop.), insofar as it is eternal, it possesses the knowledge of God, which knowledge is necessarily adequate (II: 46); hence the mind, insofar as it is eternal, is capable of knowing everything which can follow from this given knowledge of God (II: 40), in other words, of knowing things by the third kind of knowledge (see Definition in II: 40 n2), whereof accordingly the mind (III: def1), insofar as it is eternal, is the adequate or formal cause of such knowledge. QED.

NOTE: In proportion, therefore, as a man is more potent in this kind of knowledge, he will be more completely conscious of himself and of God; in other words, he will be more perfect and blessed, as will appear more clearly in the sequel. But we must here observe that, although we are already certain that the mind is eternal, insofar as it conceives things under the form of eternity, yet, in order that what we wish to show may be more readily explained and better understood, we will consider the mind itself, as though it had just begun to exist and to understand things under the form of eternity, as indeed we have done hitherto; this we may do without any danger of error, so long as we are careful not to draw any conclusion, unless our premises are plain.

PROP. 32:

Whatsoever we understand by the third kind of knowledge, we take delight in, and our delight is accompanied by the idea of God as cause.

PROOF: From this kind of knowledge arises the highest possible mental acquiescence, that is (III: emot25), pleasure, and this acquiescence is accompanied by the idea of the mind itself (V: 27), and consequently (V: 30) the idea also of God as cause. QED.

COROLLARY: From the third kind of knowledge necessarily arises the intellectual love of God. From this kind of knowledge arises pleasure accompanied by the idea of God as cause, that is (III: emot6), the love of God; not insofar as we imagine him as present (V: 29), but insofar as we understand him to be eternal; this is what I call the intellectual love of God.

PROP. 33:

The intellectual love of God, which arises from the third kind of knowledge, is eternal.

PROOF: The third kind of knowledge is eternal (V: 31; I: ax3); therefore (by the same Axiom) the love which arises therefrom is also necessarily eternal. QED.

NOTE: Although this love towards God has (by the foregoing Prop.) no beginning, it yet possesses all the perfections of love, just as though it had arisen as we feigned in the Coroll. of the last Prop. Nor is there here any difference, except that the mind possesses as eternal those same perfections which we feigned to accrue to it, and they are accompanied by the idea of God as eternal cause. If pleasure consists in the transition to a greater perfection, assuredly blessedness must consist in the mind being endowed with perfection itself.

PROP. 34:

The mind is, only while the body endures, subject to those emotions which are attributable to passions.

PROOF: Imagination is the idea wherewith the mind contemplates a thing as present (II: 17 n); yet this idea indicates rather the present disposition of the human body than the nature of the external thing (II: 16 c2). Therefore emotion (see III: General Definition of Emotions) is imagination, insofar as it indicates the present disposition of the body; therefore (V: 21) the mind is, only while the body endures, subject to emotions which are attributable to passions. QED.

COROLLARY: Hence it follows that no love save intellectual love is eternal.

NOTE: If we look to men's general opinion, we shall see that they are indeed conscious of the eternity of their mind, but that they confuse eternity with duration, and ascribe it to the imagination or the memory which they believe to remain after death.

PROP. 35:

God loves himself with an infinite intellectual love.

PROOF: God is absolutely infinite (I: def6), that is (II: def6), the nature of God rejoices in infinite perfection; and such rejoicing is (II: 3) accompanied by the idea of himself, that is (I: 11 and def1), the idea of his own cause: now this is what we have (in V: 32 c) described as intellectual love.

PROP. 36:

The intellectual love of the mind towards God is that very love of God whereby God loves himself, not insofar as he is infinite, but insofar as he can be explained through the essence of the human mind regarded under the form of eternity; in other words, the intellectual love of the mind towards God is part of the infinite love wherewith God loves himself.

PROOF: This love of the mind must be referred to the activities of the mind (V: 32 c; III: 3); it is itself, indeed, an activity whereby the mind regards itself accompanied by the idea of God as cause (V: 32 and c); that is (I: 25 c; II: 11 c), an activity whereby God, insofar as he can be explained through the human mind, regards himself accompanied by the idea of himself; therefore (by the last Prop.), this love of the mind is part of the infinite love wherewith God loves himself. QED.

COROLLARY: Hence it follows that God, insofar as he loves himself, loves man, and, consequently, that the love of God towards men and the intellectual love of the mind towards God are identical.

NOTE: From what has been said we clearly understand, wherein our salvation, or blessedness, or freedom, consists: namely, in the constant and eternal love towards God, or in God's love towards men. This love or blessedness is, in the Bible, called Glory, and not undeservedly. For whether this love be referred to God or to the mind, it may rightly be called acquiescence of spirit, which (III: emot25, emot30) is not really distinguished from glory. Insofar as it is referred to God, it is (V: 35) pleasure, if we may still use that term, accompanied by the idea of itself, and, insofar as it is referred to the mind, it is the same (V: 27).

Again, since the essence of our mind consists solely in knowledge, whereof the beginning and the foundation is God (I: 15; II: 47 n), it becomes clear to us, in what manner and way our mind, as to its essence and existence, follows from the divine nature and constantly depends on God. I have thought it worthwhile here to call attention to this, in order to show by this example how the knowledge of particular things, which I have called intuitive or of the third kind (II: 40 n2), is potent, and more powerful than the universal knowledge, which I have styled knowledge of the second kind. For, although in Part I I showed in general terms, that all things (and consequently, also, the human mind) depend as to their essence and existence on God, yet that demonstration, though legitimate and placed beyond the chances of doubt, does not affect our mind so much, as when the same conclusion is derived from the actual essence of some particular thing, which we say depends on God.

PROP. 37:

There is nothing in nature, which is contrary to this intellectual love, or which can take it away.

PROOF: This intellectual love follows necessarily from the nature of the mind, insofar as the latter is regarded through the nature of God as an eternal truth (V: 33, 29). If, therefore, there should be anything which would be contrary to this love, that thing would be contrary to that which is true; consequently, that, which should be able to take away this love, would cause that which is true to be false; an obvious absurdity. Therefore there is nothing in nature which, etc. QED.

NOTE: The Axiom of Part IV has reference to particular things, insofar as they are regarded in relation to a given time and place: of this, I think, no one can doubt.

PROP. 38:

In proportion as the mind understands more things by the second and third kind of knowledge, it is less subject to those emotions which are evil, and stands in less fear of death.

PROOF: The mind's essence consists in knowledge (II: 11); therefore, in proportion as the mind understands more things by the second and third kinds of knowledge, the greater will be the part of it that endures (V: 29, 23), and, consequently (by the last Prop.), the greater will be the part that is not touched by the emotions, which are contrary to our nature, or in other words, evil (IV: 30). Thus, in proportion as the mind understands more things by the second and third kinds of knowledge, the greater will be the part of it, that remains unimpaired, and, consequently, less subject to emotions, etc. QED.

NOTE: Hence we understand that point which I touched on in IV: 39 n, and which I promised to explain in this Part; namely, that death becomes less hurtful, in proportion as the mind's clear and distinct knowledge is greater, and, consequently, in proportion as the mind loves God more. Again, since from the third kind of knowledge arises the highest possible acquiescence (V: 27), it follows that the human mind can attain to being of such a nature, that the part thereof which we have shown to perish with the body (V: 21) should be of little importance when compared with the part which endures. But I will soon treat of the subject at greater length.

Prop. 39:

He, who possesses a body capable of the greatest number of activities, possesses a mind whereof the greatest part is eternal.

PROOF: He, who possesses a body capable of the greatest number of activities, is least agitated by those emotions which are evil (IV: 38)—that is (IV: 30), by those emotions which are contrary to our nature; therefore (V: 10), he possesses the power of arranging and associating the modifications of the body according to the intellectual order, and, consequently, of bringing it about, that all the modifications of the body should be referred to the idea of God; whence it will come to pass that (V: 15) he will be affected with love towards God, which (V: 16) must occupy or constitute the chief part of the mind; therefore (V: 33), such a man will possess a mind whereof the chief part is eternal. QED.

NOTE: Since human bodies are capable of the greatest number of activities, there is no doubt but that they may be of such a nature, that they may be referred to minds possessing a great knowledge of themselves and of God, and whereof the greatest or chief part is eternal, and, therefore, that they should scarcely fear death. But, in order that this may be understood more clearly, we must here call to mind, that we live in a state of perpetual variation, and, according as we are changed for the better or the worse, we are called happy or unhappy.

For he, who, from being an infant or a child, becomes a corpse, is called unhappy; whereas it is set down to happiness, if we have been able to live through the whole period of life with a sound mind in a sound body. And, in reality, he, who, as in the case of an infant or a child, has a body capable of very few activities, and depending, for the most part, on external causes, has a mind which, considered in itself alone, is scarcely conscious of itself, or of God, or of things; whereas, he, who has a body capable of very many activities, has a mind which, considered in itself alone, is highly conscious of itself, of God, and of things. In this life, therefore, we primarily endeavor to bring it about, that the body of a child, insofar as its nature allows and conduces thereto, may be changed into something else capable of very many activities, and referable to a mind which is highly conscious of itself, of God, and of things; and we desire so to change it, that what is referred to its imagination and memory may become insignificant, in comparison with its intellect, as I have already said in the note to the last Proposition.

PROP. 40:

In proportion as each thing possesses more of perfection, so is it more active, and less passive; and, vice versa, in proportion as it is more active, so is it more perfect.

PROOF: In proportion as each thing is more perfect, it possesses more of reality (II: def6), and, consequently (III: 3 and n), it is to that extent more active and less passive. This demonstration may be reversed, and thus prove that, in proportion as a thing is more active, so is it more perfect. QED.

COROLLARY: Hence it follows that the part of the mind which endures, be it great or small, is more perfect than the rest. For the eternal part of the mind (V: 23, 29) is the understanding, through which alone we are said to act (III: 3); the part which we have shown to perish is the imagination (V: 21), through which only we are said to be passive (III: 3; General Definition of the Emotions); therefore, the former, be it great or small, is more perfect than the latter. QED.

NOTE: Such are the doctrines which I had purposed to set forth concerning the mind, insofar as it is regarded without relation to the body; whence, as also from I: 21 and other places, it is plain that our mind, insofar as it understands, is an eternal mode of thinking, which is determined by another eternal mode of thinking, and this other by a third, and so on to infinity; so that all taken together at once constitute the eternal and infinite intellect of God.

PROP. 41:

Even if we did not know that our mind is eternal, we should still consider as of primary importance piety and religion, and generally all things which, in Part IV, we showed to be attributable to courage and high-mindedness.

PROOF: The first and only foundation of virtue, or the rule of right living is (IV: 22 c, 24) seeking one's own true interest. Now, while we determined what reason prescribes as useful, we took no account of the mind's eternity, which has only become known to us in this Fifth Part. Although we were ignorant at that time that the mind is eternal, we nevertheless stated that the qualities attributable to courage and high-mindedness are of primary importance. Therefore, even if we were still ignorant of this doctrine, we should yet put the aforesaid precepts of reason in the first place. QED.

NOTE: The general belief of the multitude seems to be different. Most people seem to believe that they are free, insofar as they may obey their lusts, and that they cede their rights, insofar as they are bound to live according to the commandments of the divine law. They therefore believe that piety, religion, and, generally, all things attributable to firmness of mind, are burdens, which, after death, they hope to lay aside, and to receive the reward for their bondage, that is, for their piety and religion; it is not only by this hope, but also, and chiefly, by the fear of being horribly punished after death, that they are induced to live according to the divine commandments, so far as their feeble and infirm spirit will carry them.

If men had not this hope and this fear, but believed that the mind perishes with the body, and that no hope of prolonged life remains for the wretches who are broken down with the burden of piety, they would return to their own inclinations, controlling everything in accordance with their lusts, and desiring to obey fortune rather than themselves. Such a course appears to me not less absurd than if a man, because he does not believe that he can by wholesome food sustain his body forever, should wish to cram himself with poisons and deadly fare; or if, because he sees that the mind is not eternal or immortal, he should prefer to be out of his mind altogether, and to live without the use of reason; these ideas are so absurd as to be scarcely worth refuting.

PROP. 42:

Blessedness is not the reward of virtue, but virtue itself; neither do we rejoice therein, because we control our lusts, but, contrariwise, because we rejoice therein, we are able to control our lusts.

PROOF: Blessedness consists in love towards God (V: 36 and n), which love springs from the third kind of knowledge (V: 32 c); therefore this love (III: 3; 59) must be referred to the mind, insofar as the latter is active; therefore (IV: def8) it is virtue itself. This was our first point. Again, in proportion as the mind rejoices more in this divine love or blessedness, so does it the more understand (V: 32); that is (V: 3 c), so much the more power has it over the emotions, and (V: 38) so much the less is it subject to those emotions which are evil; therefore, in proportion as the mind rejoices in this divine love or blessedness, so has it the power of controlling lusts. And, since human power in controlling the emotions consists solely in the understanding, it follows that no one rejoices in blessedness, because he has controlled his lusts, but, contrariwise, his power of controlling his lusts arises from this blessedness itself. QED.

Book Three

Letters

Spinoza to Henry Oldenburg
[On Miracles]

Distinguished Sir,

I RECEIVED ON SATURDAY last your very short letter dated 15th Nov. 1675. In it you merely indicate the points in the theological treatise, which have given pain to readers, whereas I had hoped to learn from it, what were the opinions which militated against the practice of religious virtue, and which you formerly mentioned. However, I will speak on the three subjects on which you desire me to disclose my sentiments, and tell you, first, that my opinion concerning God differs widely from that which is ordinarily defended by modern Christians. For I hold that God is of all things the cause immanent, as the phrase is, not transient. I say that all things are in God and move in God, thus agreeing with Paul, and, perhaps, with all the ancient philosophers, though the phraseology may be different; I will even venture to affirm that I agree with all the ancient Hebrews, insofar as one may judge from their traditions, though these are in many ways corrupted. The supposition of some, that I endeavor to prove in the *Tractatus Theologico-Politicus* the unity of God and Nature (meaning by the latter a certain mass or corporeal matter), is wholly erroneous.

As regards miracles, I am of opinion that the revelation of God can only be established by the wisdom of the doctrine, not by miracles, or in other words by ignorance. This I have shown at sufficient length in Chapter VI concerning miracles. I will here only add that I make this chief distinction between religion and superstition, that the latter is founded on ignorance, the former on knowledge; this, I take it, is the reason why Christians are distinguished from the rest of the world, not by faith, nor by charity, nor by the other fruits of the Holy Spirit, but solely by their opinions, inasmuch as they defend their cause, like everyone else, by miracles, that is by ignorance, which is the source of all malice; thus they turn a faith, which may be true, into superstition. . . .

I will tell you that I do not think it necessary for salvation to know Christ according to the flesh: but with regard to the Eternal Son of God, that is the Eternal Wisdom of God, which has manifested itself in all things and especially in the human mind, and above all in Christ Jesus, the case is far otherwise. For without this no one can come to a state of blessedness, inasmuch as it alone teaches what is true or false, good or evil. And, inasmuch as this wisdom was made especially manifest through Jesus Christ, as I have said, His disciples preached it, insofar as it was revealed to them through Him, and thus showed that they could rejoice in that spirit of Christ more than the rest of mankind. The doctrines added by certain churches, such as that God took upon Himself human nature, I have expressly said that I do not understand; in fact, to speak the truth, they seem to me no less absurd than would a statement that a circle had taken upon itself the nature of a square. This, I think, will be sufficient explanation of my opinions concerning the three points mentioned. Whether it will be satisfactory to Christians, you will know better than I. Farewell. . . .

LETTER 23

Spinoza to Henry Oldenburg
[On Miracles and Christianity]

. . . I have taken miracles and ignorance as equivalent terms, because those who endeavor to establish God's existence and the truth of religion by means of miracles seek to prove the obscure by what is more obscure and completely unknown, thus introducing a new sort of argument, the reduction, not to the impossible, as the phrase is, but to ignorance. But, if I mistake not, I have sufficiently explained my opinion on miracles in the *Theologico-Political Treatise*. I will only add here, that if you will reflect on the facts, that Christ did not appear to the council, nor to Pilate, nor to any unbeliever, but only to the faithful; also that God has neither right hand nor left, but is by His essence not in a particular spot, but everywhere; that matter is everywhere the same; that God does not manifest himself in the imaginary space supposed to be outside the world; and lastly, that the frame of the human body is kept within due limits solely by the weight of the air; you will readily see that this apparition of Christ is not unlike that wherewith God appeared to Abraham, when the latter saw men whom he invited to dine with him. But, you will say, all the Apostles thoroughly believed that Christ rose from the dead and really ascended to heaven: I do not deny it. Abraham, too, believed that God had dined with him, and all the Israelites believed that God descended, surrounded with fire, from heaven to Mount Sinai, and there spoke directly with them; whereas, these apparitions or revelations and many others like them were adapted to the understanding and opinions of those men to whom God wished thereby to reveal His will. I therefore conclude that the resurrection of Christ from the dead was in reality spiritual, and that to the faithful alone, according to their understanding, it was revealed that Christ was endowed with eternity and had risen from the dead (using *dead* in the sense in which Christ said, "Let the dead bury their dead."), giving by His life and death a matchless example of holiness. Moreover, He to this extent raises his disciples from the dead, insofar as they follow the example of His own life and death. It would not be difficult to explain the whole Gospel doctrine on this hypothesis. Nay, 1 Cor. ch. XV cannot be explained on any other, nor can Paul's arguments be understood: if we follow the common interpretation, they appear weak and can easily be refuted; not to mention the fact that Christians interpret spiritually all those doctrines which the Jews accepted literally. I join with you in acknowledging human weakness. But on the other hand, I venture to ask you whether we "human pigmies" possess sufficient knowledge of nature to be able to lay down the limits of its force and power or to say that a given thing surpasses that power? No one could go so far without arrogance. We may, therefore, without presumption, explain miracles as far as possible by natural causes. When we cannot explain them, nor even prove their impossibility, we may well suspend our judgment about them, and establish religion, as I have said, solely by the wisdom of its doctrines. You think that the texts in John's Gospel and in Hebrews are inconsistent with what I advance because you measure oriental phrases by the standards of European speech; though John wrote his gospel in Greek, he wrote it as a Hebrew. However this may be, do you believe, when Scripture says that God manifested Himself in a cloud, or that He dwelt in the tabernacle or the temple, that God actually assumed the nature of a cloud, a tabernacle, or a temple? Yet the utmost that Christ says of Himself is that He is the Temple of God, because, as I said before, God had specially manifested Himself in Christ. John, wishing to express the same truth more forcibly, said that "the Word was made flesh." But I have said enough on the subject.

LETTER 25

Spinoza to Henry Oldenburg
[On God, Miracles, and Christianity]
February 7, 1676

... I do not think it necessary here to remind you that Scripture, when it says that God is angry with sinners and that He is a Judge who takes cognizance of human actions, passes sentence on them, and judges them, is speaking humanly, and in a way adapted to the received opinion of the masses, inasmuch as its purpose is not to teach philosophy, nor to render men wise, but to make them obedient.

How, by taking miracles and ignorance as equivalent terms, I reduce God's power and man's knowledge within the same limits, I am unable to discern.

For the rest, I accept Christ's passion, death, and burial literally, as you do, but His resurrection I understand allegorically. I admit, that it is related by the Evangelists in such detail, that we cannot deny that they themselves believed Christ's body to have risen from the dead and ascended to heaven, in order to sit at the right hand of God, or that they believed that Christ might have been seen by unbelievers, if they had happened to be at hand, in the places where He appeared to His disciples; but in these matters they might, without injury to Gospel teaching, have been deceived, as was the case with other prophets mentioned in my last letter. But Paul, to whom Christ afterwards appeared, rejoices that he knew Christ not after the flesh, but after the spirit. Farewell, honorable Sir, and believe me yours in all affection and zeal.

LETTER 28

Spinoza to Simon de Vries
[About A Priori Thinking]

Respected Friend,

You ask me if we have need of experience in order to know whether the definition of a given attribute is true. To this I answer that we never need experience except in cases when the existence of the thing cannot be inferred from its definition, as, for instance, the existence of modes (which cannot be inferred from their definition); experience is not needed, when

the existence of the things in question is not distinguished from their essence, and is therefore inferred
from their definition. This can never be taught us by
any experience, for experience does not teach us any
essences of things; the utmost it can do is to set our
mind thinking about definite essences only. Wherefore, when the existence of attributes does not differ
from their essence, no experience is capable of attaining it for us. . . .

LETTER 32

Spinoza to William de Blyenbergh
[On Friendship]
January 5, 1665
Long Orchard, near Amsterdam

Unknown Friend,

I received, at Schiedam, on the 26th of December,
your letter dated the 12th of December, enclosed
in another written on the 24th of the same month.
I gather from it your fervent love of truth and your
making it the aim of all your studies. This compelled
me, though by no means otherwise unwilling, not
only to grant your petition by answering all the questions you have sent, or may in future send, to the best
of my ability, but also to impart to you everything in
my power, which can conduce to further knowledge
and sincere friendship. So far as in me lies, I value,
above all other things out of my own control, the

joining hands of friendship with men who are sincere lovers of truth. I believe that nothing in the world, of things outside our own control, brings more peace than the possibility of affectionate intercourse with such men; it is just as impossible that the love we bear them can be disturbed (inasmuch as it is founded on the desire each feels for the knowledge of truth) as that truth once perceived should not be assented to. It is, moreover, the highest and most pleasing source of happiness derivable from things not under our own control. Nothing save truth has power closely to unite different feelings and dispositions. I say nothing of the very great advantages which it brings, lest I should detain you too long on a subject which, doubtless, you know already. I have said thus much in order to show you better how gladly I shall embrace this and any future opportunity of serving you....

LETTER 40

Spinoza to Christian Huyghens
[On God]
April 10, 1666
Voorburg

Distinguished Sir,

In your last letter, written on March 30th, you have excellently elucidated the point, which was somewhat obscure to me in your letter of February 10th. As I now know your opinion, I will set forth the state of the question as you conceive it; whether there be only a single Being who subsists by his own sufficiency or force? I not only affirm this to be so, but also undertake to prove it from the fact that the nature of such a Being necessarily involves existence; perhaps it may also be readily proved from the understanding of God (as I set forth, "Principles of Cartesian Philosophy," I. Prop. 1.), or from others of His attributes. Before treating of the subject I will briefly show, as preliminaries, what properties must be possessed by a Being including necessary existence. To wit:

1. It must be eternal. For if a definite duration be assigned to it, it would beyond that definite duration be conceived as nonexistent, or as not involving necessary existence, which would be contrary to its definition.

2. It must be simple, not made up of parts. For parts must in nature and knowledge be prior to the whole they compose: this could not be the case with regard to that which is eternal.

3. It cannot be conceived as determinate, but only as infinite. For, if the nature of the said Being were determinate, and conceived as determinate, that nature would beyond the said limits be conceived as nonexistent, which again is contrary to its definition.

4. It is indivisible. For if it were divisible, it could be divided into parts, either of the

same or of different nature. If the latter, it could be destroyed and so not exist, which is contrary to its definition; if the former, each part would in itself include necessary existence, and thus one part could exist without others, and consequently be conceived as so existing. Hence the nature of the Being would be comprehended as finite, which, by what has been said, is contrary to its definition. Thus we see that, in attempting to ascribe to such a Being any imperfection, we straightway fall into contradictions. For, whether the imperfection which we wish to assign to the said Being be situate in any defect, or in limitations possessed by its nature, or in any change which it might, through deficiency of power, undergo from external causes, we are always brought back to the contradiction that a nature which involves necessary existence, does not exist, or does not necessarily exist. I conclude, therefore,

5. That everything, which includes necessary existence, cannot have in itself any imperfection, but must express pure perfection.

6. Further, since only from perfection can it come about that any Being should exist by its own sufficiency and force, it follows

that if we assume a Being to exist by its own nature, but not to express all perfections, we must further suppose that another Being exists, which does comprehend in itself all perfections. For, if the less powerful Being exists by its own sufficiency, how much more must the more powerful so exist?

Lastly, to deal with the question, I affirm that there can only be a single Being, of which the existence belongs to its nature; such a Being which possesses in itself all perfections I will call God. If there be any Being to whose nature existence belongs, such a Being can contain in itself no imperfection, but must (by my fifth premise) express every perfection; therefore, the nature of such a Being seems to belong to God (whose existence we are bound to affirm by Premise VI), inasmuch as He has in Himself all perfections and no imperfections. Nor can it exist externally to God. For if, externally to God, there existed one and the same nature involving necessary existence, such nature would be twofold; but this, by what we have just shown, is absurd. Therefore there is nothing save God, but there is a single God, that involves necessary existence, which was to be proved.

Such, distinguished Sir, are the arguments I can now produce for demonstrating this question. I hope I may also demonstrate to you that I am, etc.

Spinoza to Christian Huyghens
[On God]
May 1666
Voorburg

Distinguished Sir,

I have been by one means or another prevented from answering sooner your letter dated 19th May. As I gather that you suspend your judgment with regard to most of the demonstration I sent you (owing, I believe, to the obscurity you find in it), I will here endeavor to explain its meaning more clearly.

First I enumerated four properties, which a Being existing by its own sufficiency or force must possess. These four, and others like them, I reduced in my fifth observation to one. Further, in order to deduce all things necessary for the demonstration from a single premise, I endeavored in my sixth observation to demonstrate the existence of God from the given hypothesis; whence, lastly, taking (as you know) nothing beyond the ordinary meaning of the terms, I drew the desired conclusion.

Such, in brief, was my purpose and such my aim. I will now explain the meaning of each step singly, and will first start with the aforesaid four properties.

In the first you find no difficulty, nor is it anything but, as in the case of the second, an axiom. By simple, I merely mean not compound, or not made up of parts differing in nature or other parts agreeing in nature. This demonstration is assuredly universal.

The sense of my third observation (that if the Being be thought, it cannot be conceived as limited by thought, but only as infinite, and similarly, if it be extension, it cannot be conceived as limited by extension) you have excellently perceived, though you say you do not perceive the conclusion; this last is based on the fact that a contradiction is involved in conceiving under the category of nonexistence anything whose definition includes or (what is the same thing) affirms existence. And since determination implies nothing positive, but only a limitation of the existence of the nature conceived as determinate, it follows that that, of which the definition affirms existence, cannot be conceived as determinate. For instance, if the term extension included necessary existence, it would be alike impossible to conceive extension without existence and existence without extension. If this were established, it would be impossible to conceive determinate extension. For, if it be conceived as determinate, it must be determined by its own nature that is by extension, and this extension, whereby it is determined, must be conceived under the category of nonexistence, which by the hypothesis is obviously a contradiction. In my fourth observation, I merely wished to show that such a Being could neither be divided into parts of the same nature or parts of a different nature, whether those of a different nature involved necessary existence or not. If, I said, we adopt the second view, the Being would be destroyed; for destruction is merely the resolution of a thing into parts so that none of them expresses the nature of the whole; if we adopt the first view, we should be in contradiction with the first three properties.

In my fifth observation, I merely asserted that perfection consists in being, and imperfection in the privation of being. I say the privation; for although extension denies of itself thought, this argues no imperfection in it. It would be an imperfection in it if it were in any degree deprived of extension, as it would be, if it were determinate; or again, if it lacked duration, position, etc.

My sixth observation you accept absolutely, and yet you say that your whole difficulty remains (inasmuch as there may be, you think, several self-existent entities of different nature; as for instance thought and extension are different and perhaps subsist by their own sufficiency). I am, therefore, forced to believe that you attribute to my observation a meaning quite different from the one intended by me. I think I can discern your interpretation of it; however, in order to save time, I will merely set forth my own meaning. I say then, as regards my sixth observation, that if we assert that anything, which is indeterminate and perfect only after its kind, exists by its own sufficiency, we must also grant the existence of a Being indeterminate and perfect absolutely; such a Being I will call God. If, for example, we wish to assert that extension or thought (which are each perfect after their kind, that is, in a given sphere of being) exists by its own sufficiency, we must grant also the existence of God, who is absolutely perfect, that is of a Being absolutely indeterminate. I would here direct attention to what I have just said with regard to the term *imperfection*; namely, that it signifies that a thing is deficient in some quality, which, nevertheless, belongs to its nature. For instance, extension can only be called imperfect in respect of duration, position, or quantity: that is, as not enduring longer, as not retaining its position, or as not being greater. It can never be called imperfect, because it does not think, inasmuch as its nature requires nothing of the kind, but consists solely in extension, that is in a certain sphere of being. Only in respect to its own sphere can it be called determinate or indeterminate, perfect or imperfect. Now, since the nature of God is not confined to a certain sphere of being, but exists in being, which is absolutely indeterminate, so His nature also demands everything which perfectly expresses being; otherwise His nature would be determinate and deficient.

This being so, it follows that there can be only one Being, namely God, who exists by His own force. If, for the sake of an illustration, we assert that extension involves existence; it is, therefore, necessary that it should be eternal and indeterminate and express absolutely no imperfection, but perfection. Hence extension will appertain to God, or will be something which in some fashion expresses the nature of God, since God is a Being, who not only in a certain respect but absolutely is in essence indeterminate and omnipotent. What we have here said by way of illustration regarding extension must be asserted of all that we ascribe a similar existence to. I, therefore, conclude as in my former letter that there is nothing external to God, but that God alone exists by His own sufficiency. I think I have said enough to show the meaning of my former letter; however, of this you will be the best judge. . . .

LETTER 47

Spinoza to I. I. (unknown person, possibly Jarig Jellis)
[Defending Spinoza's Philosophy]
February 17, 1671
The Hague

Most Courteous Sir,

When Professor N. N. visited me the other day, he told me that my *Theologico-Political Treatise* has been translated into Dutch, and that someone, whose name he did not know, was about printing it. With regard to this, I earnestly beg you to inquire carefully into the business, and, if possible, stop the printing. This is the request not only of myself, but of many of my friends and acquaintances, who would be sorry to see the book placed under an interdict, as it undoubtedly would be, if published in Dutch. I do not doubt but that you will do this service to me and the cause.

One of my friends sent me a short time since a pamphlet called "Homo Politicus," of which I had heard much. I have read it, and find it to be the most pernicious work which men could devise or invent. Rank and riches are the author's highest good; he adapts his doctrine accordingly, and shows the means to acquire them; to wit, by inwardly rejecting all religion, and outwardly professing whatever best serves his own advancement, also by keeping faith with no one, except insofar as he himself is profited thereby. For the rest, to feign, to make promises and break them, to lie, to swear falsely, and many such like practices call forth his highest praises. When I had finished reading the book, I debated whether I should write a pamphlet indirectly aimed against its author, wherein I should treat of the highest good and show the troubled and wretched condition of those who are covetous of rank and riches; finally proving by very plain reasoning and many examples that the insatiable desire for rank and riches must bring and has brought ruin to states.

How much better and more excellent than the doctrines of the aforesaid writer are the reflections of Thales of Miletus appears from the following. All the goods of friends, he says, are in common; wise men are the friends of the gods, and all things belong to the gods; therefore all things belong to the wise. Thus in a single sentence, this wisest of men accounts himself most rich, rather by nobly despising riches than by sordidly seeking them. In other passages he shows that the wise lack riches, not from necessity, but from choice. For when his friends reproached him with his poverty he answered, "Do you wish me to show you that I could acquire what I deem unworthy of my labor, but you so diligently seek?" On their answering in the affirmative, he hired every oil-press in the whole of Greece (for being a distinguished astrologer he knew that the olive harvest would be as abundant as in previous years it had been scanty), and sub-let at his own price what he had hired for a very small sum, thus acquiring in a single year a large fortune, which he bestowed liberally as he had gained it industriously, etc.

LETTER 49

Spinoza to Isaac Orobio
[Defending Spinoza's Philosophy against
Charge of Atheism]
1671
The Hague

Most Learned Sir,

You doubtless wonder why I have kept you so long waiting. I could hardly bring myself to reply to the pamphlet of that person, which you thought fit to send me; indeed I only do so now because of my promise. However, in order as far as possible to humor my feelings, I will fulfill my engagement in as few words as I can, and will briefly show how perversely he has interpreted my meaning; whether through malice or through ignorance I cannot readily say. But to the matter in hand.

First he says, *"That it is of little moment to know what nation I belong to, or what sort of life I lead."* Truly, if he had known, he would not so easily have persuaded himself that I teach Atheism. For Atheists are wont greedily to covet rank and riches, which I have always despised, as all who know me are aware. Again, in order to smooth his path to the object he has in view, he says that, *"I am possessed of no mean talents,"* so that he may, forsooth, more easily convince his readers that I have knowingly and cunningly with evil intent argued for the cause of the deists, in order to discredit it. This contention sufficiently shows that he has not understood my reasons. For who could be so cunning and clever as to be able to advance under false pretences so many and such good reasons for a doctrine which he did not believe in? Who will pass for an honest writer in the eyes of a man that thinks one may argue as soundly for fiction as for truth? But after all I am not astonished. Descartes was formerly served in the same way by Voët, and the most honorable writers are constantly thus treated.

He goes on to say, "*In order to shun the reproach of superstition, he seems to me to have thrown off all religion.*" What this writer means by religion and what by superstition, I know not. But I would ask, whether a man throws off all religion who maintains that God must be acknowledged as the highest good, and must, as such, be loved with a free mind? Or, again, that the reward of virtue is virtue itself, while the punishment of folly and weakness is folly itself? Or, lastly, that every man ought to love his neighbor, and to obey the commands of the supreme power? Such doctrines I have not only expressly stated but have also demonstrated them by very solid reasoning. However, I think I see the mud wherein this person sticks. He finds nothing in virtue and the understanding in themselves to please him, but would prefer to live in accordance with his passions, if it were not for the single obstacle that he fears punishment. He abstains from evil actions, and obeys the divine commands like a slave, with unwillingness and hesitation, expecting as the reward of his bondage to be recompensed by God with gifts far more pleasing than divine love and greater in proportion to his dislike to goodness and consequent unwillingness to practice it. Hence it comes to pass that he believes that all who are not restrained by this fear lead a life of license and throw off all religion. But this I pass over, and proceed to the deduction, whereby he wishes to show that "*with*

covert and disguised arguments I teach atheism." The
foundation of his reasoning is that he thinks I take
away freedom from God and subject Him to fate. This
is flatly false. For I have maintained that all things follow by inevitable necessity from the nature of God, in
the same way as all maintain that it follows from the
nature of God that He understands Himself: no one
denies that this latter consequence follows necessarily from the divine nature, yet no one conceives that
God is constrained by any fate; they believe that He
understands Himself with entire freedom, though
necessarily. I find nothing here that cannot be perceived by everyone; if, nevertheless, my adversary
thinks that these arguments are advanced with evil
intent, what does he think of his own Descartes, who
asserted that nothing is done by us, which has not
been pre-ordained by God, nay, that we are newly created as it were by God every moment, though none-
theless we act according to our own free will? This, as
Descartes himself confesses, no one can understand.

Further, this inevitable necessity in things destroys
neither divine laws nor human. For moral principles,
whether they have received from God the form of laws
or not, are nevertheless divine and salutary. Whether
we accept the good, which follows from virtue and
the divine love, as given us by God as a judge, or as
emanating from the necessity of the divine nature, it
is not in either case more or less to be desired; nor

are the evils which follow from evil actions less to be feared, because they follow necessarily: finally, whether we act under necessity or freedom, we are in either case led by hope and fear. Wherefore the assertion is false, "*that I maintain that there is no room left for precepts and commands.*" Or as he goes on to say, "*that there is no expectation of reward or punishment, since all things are ascribed to fate, and are said to flow with inevitable necessity from God.*"

I do not here inquire why it is the same or almost the same to say that all things necessarily flow from God, as to say that God is universal; but I would have you observe the insinuation which he not less maliciously subjoins, "*that I wish that men should practice virtue, not because of the precepts and law of God, or through hope of reward and fear of punishment, but,*" etc. Such a sentiment you will assuredly not find anywhere in my treatise: on the contrary, I have expressly stated in Chap. IV that the sum of the divine law (which, as I have said in Chap. II, has been divinely inscribed on our hearts), and its chief precept is, to love God as the highest good; not, indeed, from the fear of any punishment, for love cannot spring from fear; nor for the love of anything which we desire for our own delight, for then we should love not God, but the object of our desire.

I have shown in the same chapter that God revealed this law to the prophets, so that, whether it received from God the form of a command, or whether we conceive it to be like God's other decrees, which involve eternal necessity and truth, it will in either case remain God's decree and a salutary principle. Whether I love God in freedom, or whether I love Him from the necessity of the divine decree, I shall nevertheless love God, and shall be in a state of salvation. Wherefore, I can now declare here that this person is one of that sort, of whom I have said at the end of my preface, that I would rather that they utterly neglected my book than that by misinterpreting it after their wont they should become hostile, and hinder others without benefiting themselves. . . .

Again, I cannot see why he says that all will adopt my opinions, who deny that reason and philosophy should be the interpreters of Scripture; I have refuted the doctrine of such persons, together with that of Maimonides.

It would take too long to review all the indications he gives of not having judged me altogether calmly. I therefore pass on to his conclusion, where he says, *"that I have no arguments left to prove, that Mahomet was not a true prophet. . . ."*

As regards the Turks and other non-Christian nations; if they worship God by the practice of justice and charity towards their neighbor, I believe that they have the spirit of Christ, and are in a state of salvation. . . .

LETTER 52

Spinoza to Godfrey Leibnitz
[Spinoza Responds to Leibnitz, who has sent
a Paper on Optics for Comment]
November 9, 1671
The Hague

Most Learned and Distinguished Sir,

I have read the paper you were kind enough to send me, and return you many thanks for the communication. I regret that I have not been able quite to follow your meaning, though you explain it sufficiently clearly, whether you think that there is any cause for making the apertures of the glasses small, except that the rays coming from a single point are not collected accurately at another single point, but in a small area which we generally call the mechanical point, and that this small area is greater or less in proportion to the size of the aperture. Further, I ask whether the lenses which you call "pandochæ" correct this fault, so that the mechanical point or small area, on which the rays coming from a single point are after refraction collected, always preserves the same proportional size, whether the aperture be small or large. If so, one may enlarge the aperture as much as one likes, and consequently these lenses will be far superior to those of any other shape known to me; if not, I hardly see why you praise them so greatly beyond common lenses. For circular lenses have everywhere the same axis; therefore, when we employ them, we must regard all the points of an object as placed in the optic axis; although all the points of the object be not at the same distance, the difference arising thence will not be perceptible, when the objects are very remote; because then the rays coming from a single point would, as they enter the glass, be regarded as parallel. I think your lenses might be of service in obtaining a more distinct representation of all the objects, when we wish to include several objects in one view, as we do, when we employ very large convex circular lenses. However, I would rather suspend my judgment about all these details, till you have more clearly explained your meaning, as I heartily beg you to do. . . .

LETTER 54

Spinoza to I. Lewis Fabritius
[Spinoza Declines a Professorship]
March 30, 1673
The Hague

Distinguished Sir,

If I had ever desired to take a professorship in any faculty, I could not have wished for any other than that which is offered to me, through you, by His Most Serene Highness the Elector Palatine, especially because of that freedom in philosophical teaching, which the most gracious prince is kind enough to grant, not to speak of the desire which I have long entertained to live under the rule of a prince whom all men admire for his wisdom.

But since it has never been my wish to teach in public, I have been unable to induce myself to accept this splendid opportunity, though I have long deliberated about it. I think, in the first place, that I should abandon philosophical research if I consented to find time for teaching young students. I think, in the second place, that I do not know the limits within which the freedom of my philosophical teaching would be confined, if I am to avoid all appearance of disturbing the publicly established religion. Religious quarrels do not arise so much from ardent zeal for religion, as from men's various dispositions and love of contradiction, which causes them to habitually distort and condemn everything, however rightly it may have been said. I have experienced these results in my private and secluded station; how much more should I have to fear them after my elevation to this post of honor.

Thus you see distinguished Sir that I am not holding back in the hope of getting something better, but through my love of quietness, which I think I can in some measure secure, if I keep away from lecturing in public. I therefore most earnestly entreat you to beg of the Most Serene Elector, that I may be allowed to consider further about this matter, and I also ask you to conciliate the favor of the most gracious prince to his most devoted admirer, thus increasing the obligations of your sincere friend,

B. de. S.

LETTER 68-B

Spinoza to G. H. Schaller
[Spinoza's Caution in Showing His Work, Even to a Very
Celebrated Fellow Philosopher]
November 18, 1675
The Hague

. . . I believe that I have an epistolary acquaintance with . . . Leibnitz. . . . But why he, who was a counselor at Frankfort, has gone to France, I do not know. As far as I could conjecture from his letters, he seemed to me a man of liberal mind, and versed in every science. But yet I think it imprudent so soon to entrust my writings to him. I should like first to know what is his business in France, and the judgment of our friend von Tschirnhausen, when he has been longer in his company, and knows his character more intimately. However, greet that friend of ours in my name, and let him command me what he pleases, if in anything I can be of service to him, and he will find me most ready to obey him in everything. . . .

LETTER 74

Spinoza to Albert Burgh
[Burgh, a Former Protégé, Has Converted to Roman
Catholicism and Now Rejects Spinoza's Ideas]
End of 1675
The Hague

. . . In every Church there are thoroughly honorable men who worship God with justice and charity. We have known many such among the Lutherans, the Reformed Church, the Mennonites, and the Enthusiasts. Not to go further, you knew your own relations, who in the time of the Duke of Alva suffered every kind of torture bravely and willingly for the sake of their religion. In fact, you must admit that personal holiness is not peculiar to the Romish Church, but common to all Churches.

As it is by this that we know "that we dwell in God and He in us" (1 Ep. John, IV. 13), it follows that what distinguishes the Romish Church from others must be something entirely superfluous, and therefore founded solely on superstition. For, as John says, justice and charity are the one sure sign of the true Catholic faith, and the true fruits of the Holy Spirit. Wherever they are found, there in truth is Christ; wherever they are absent, Christ is absent also. For only by the Spirit of Christ can we be led to the love of justice and charity. . . .

But I return to your letter, which you begin, by lamenting that I allow myself to be ensnared by the prince of evil spirits. Pray take heart, and recollect yourself. When you had the use of your faculties, you were wont, if I mistake not, to worship an Infinite God, by Whose efficacy all things absolutely come to pass and are preserved; now you dream of a prince, God's enemy, who against God's will ensnares and deceives very many men (rarely good ones, to be sure), whom God thereupon hands over to this master of wickedness to be tortured eternally. The Divine justice therefore allows the devil to deceive men and remain unpunished; but it by no means allows to remain unpunished the men, who have been by that self-same devil miserably deceived and ensnared. . . .

. . . I do not presume that I have found the best philosophy; I know that I understand the true philosophy. If you ask in what way I know it, I answer: In the same way as you know that the three angles of a triangle are equal to two right angles; that this is sufficient, will be denied by no one whose brain is sound, and who does not go dreaming of evil spirits inspiring us with false ideas like the true. For the truth is the index of itself and of what is false. . . .

Index

E